WINNING
BASKETBALL DRILLS

ABOUT THE AUTHORS

Kenneth W. Atkins is head basketball coach at King's College in Wilkes Barre, Pennsylvania. He earned a secondary education degree at the University of Delaware where he served as student aide in the basketball program. Mr. Atkins had a stint as the top assistant coach at Widener University in Chester, PA, before serving as an assistant coach at the University of Arizona. While at Arizona, he earned his master's in secondary education. Mr. Atkins has directed several highly successful summer basketball camps: Mr. Basketball Camp, Pocono Mountains, PA; Canadensis Basketball Camp, Pocono Mountains, PA; Bill McDonough's Basketball Day Camps, Philadelphia, PA; and Ken Atkins' Basketball Day Camp, King's College, Wilkes Barre, PA.

Ronald G. Rainey is head basketball coach at the University of Delaware in Newark, Delaware. He has more than twenty-three years of coaching experience, including eighteen as head coach at the high school and college levels. Mr. Rainey has spent the past eight years leading the Fightin' Blue Hens of Delaware, where he is also an Assistant Professor in the College of Physical Education and Athletics. He has directed the Blue Hen Basketball Camp, at the University of Delaware, for the past seven summers. During this time he has been able to lecture and clinic at other outstanding summer camps on the East Coast. He has been active in committee work as a member of the National Association of Basketball Coaches for eight years.

WINNING
BASKETBALL
DRILLS

Ken Atkins and Ron Rainey

Parker Publishing Company, Inc.
West Nyack, New York

10   9   8   7

Library of Congress Cataloging in Publication Data

Atkins, Kenneth W.,
  Winning basketball drills.
  1. Basketball—Coaching.   I. Rainey, Ronald G.,
1936–   II. Title.
GV885.3.A88   1985   796.32'32   84-22674

ISBN 0-13-960618-1

Printed in the United States of America

CONTENTS

5 DEFENSIVE DRILLS

6 SHOOTING DRILLS

7 FAST-BREAK DRILLS

8 FREE-THROW DRILLS

9 INSIDE MOVES

10 LAY-UP DRILLS

11 PASSING DRILLS

12 OFFENSIVE MOVE DRILLS_____

13 REBOUNDING DRILLS_____

14 COMPETITIVE DRILLS_____

15 STATION DRILLS_____

HOW THIS BOOK
WILL HELP YOU

Our coaching experience has shown that many veteran coaches have favorite drills but fail to organize them. They may thus emphasize drills in only one area of the game over others. We have also found that most beginning or inexperienced coaches have no single reference for drills covering all aspects of the game. Coaching publications do offer articles on a wide range of drills, but although these articles are often quite helpful, the interested coach must either memorize the drill or file each article away for later use. It is in these cases where we believe this book will be helpful as a comprehensive reference for drills in all areas of the game.

What we have attempted in this book is to categorize all the drills we have used or have seen used by other coaches. We have accumulated drills from playing days, coaching magazines and books, coaching clinics, basketball camps, and conversations with other coaches. The summer-camp experience was especially helpful because of the length of time spent on fundamentals and the constant exchange of ideas among coaches.

As these drills were gathered, they were placed in categories in order to make this book an easy reference for coaches on all levels of the game. The categories are agility, conditioning, ball handling, passing, lay-ups, shooting, defense, offensive moves, post moves, rebounding, competitive, and station drills. Of course, most drills are multipurpose and could be placed in several categories. For example, a defensive drill might also include offensive moves, shooting, inside positioning, or rebounding. In cases such as these, drills were placed in the skill category that we thought received the most emphasis.

The result of this process is more than 270 drills covering all aspects of the game of basketball. Each drill is briefly explained in terms of purpose, procedure, number of personnel required, equipment and space needed, coaching tips, and drill duration. When appropriate, diagrams clearly illustrate the procedures. We have included an appendix for each of the major areas of fundamentals (offensive, defensive, and fast-break). They are available for use by the coach in order to check the basic basketball fundamentals and key teaching points involved in a drill.

We hope you will find this collection of drills a valuable aid to your coaching. Good luck!

AGILITY DRILLS

JUMP-A-LINE DRILL

Purpose: To improve foot speed and endurance.

Number of Personnel: Any number of players and a coach or manager.

Equipment and Facilities: Any line or lines on the basketball court and a stopwatch.

Procedure: Players should pick any line on the court—sideline, baseline, foul line, etc. They next place feet together on one side of the line

(example:  line).

For a given time period each player jumps back and forth across the line as many times as he or she possibly can. The player's feet should remain together and never touch the line. The coach may wish to do two or three sets. Players should count the number of times they cross the line and try to increase it each time they perform the drill

Time: At start, drill should be done for 30 seconds. It may be gradually increased to a full minute.

Coaching Points: Make sure that players maintain balance, keeping head up and eyes looking forward.

JUMP-THE-BOXES DRILL

Purpose: To improve foot speed and agility.

Number of Personnel: Any number of players and a coach or manager.

1

Equipment and Facilities: Place tape on the floor to set up boxes as shown in Diagram 1.1.

Procedure: Players begin at Box 1 and continue through the series of boxes (see Diagram 1.1). They first do drill jumping and keeping feet together, landing with both feet in each box. Second time through, each player will jump on just the right foot. The third time, each player uses only the left foot. For the final sequence, players jump and turn a complete 360°, landing with both feet in the desired box. Players should proceed as quickly as possible.

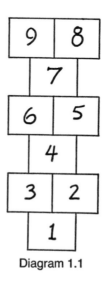

Diagram 1.1

Time: As long as it takes to complete the drill the number of times desired by the coach.

Coaching Points: Be sure that players maintain balance and be as quick as possible, keeping knees flexed.

AGILITY DRILL #1

Purpose: To improve hand reaction speed.

Number of Personnel: Any number of players and a coach or manager.

Equipment and Facilities: A whistle is needed by the coach or manager.

Procedure: Players assume a defensive stance. At the sound of the whistle, they clap their hands at the right shoulder and then at the left knee as quickly as possible and return to their stance. At the next whistle they change to left shoulder and right knee.

Time: Whatever time the coach desires.

Coaching Points: Players maintain defensive stance with head and eyes forward and react as quickly as possible.

AGILITY DRILL #2

Purpose: To improve hand reaction speed.

Number of Personnel: Any number of players and a coach or manager.

Equipment and Facilities: Coach or manager should have a whistle.

Procedure: Players assume a defensive stance. At the whistle, they clap hands in front of them and then behind their backs as quickly as possible. Return to defensive stance. Players should repeat process at each whistle.

Time: Whatever time the coach desires.

Coaching Points: Players maintain defensive stance with head and eyes forward and react as quickly as possible. Quickness is the key.

AGILITY DRILL #3

Purpose: To improve reaction time; to increase vertical jumping ability.

Number of Personnel: Any number of players and a coach or manager.

Equipment and Facilities: Coach or manager needs a whistle.

Procedure: At each whistle players jump up, touching their knees to their chests.

Time: Coach determines duration.

Coaching Points: On landing, players should be on balance and ready to repeat the jump.

AGILITY DRILL #4

Purpose: To improve reaction time; to increase vertical jumping ability.

Number of Personnel: Any number of players and a coach or manager.

Equipment and Facilities: Coach or manager must have a whistle.

Procedure: On each whistle, players jump and touch their feet to their buttocks.

Time: Whatever time the coach desires.

Coaching Points: On landing, players should be on balance and ready to repeat the jump.

AGILITY DRILL #5

Purpose: To improve reaction time; to increase vertical jumping ability.

Number of Personnel: Any number of players and a coach or manager.

Equipment and Facilities: A whistle for the coach or manager.

Procedure: At the first whistle, players jump and touch their knees to their chests. At the next whistle, they kick their feet up to touch their buttocks. Players should try to perform drill as quickly as possible.

Time: Coach determines duration.

Coaching Points: Players on landing should be on balance and ready to repeat the jumps.

AGILITY DRILL #6

Purpose: To improve hand-foot coordination; to improve foot speed; for use as a conditioner.

Number of Personnel: Any number of players.

Equipment and Facilities: One rope for each player.

Procedure: Players do a jump-rope routine in any one or combination of the following steps: just on left foot, just on right foot, both feet, left foot fast, right foot fast. The sixth step—jumping as fast as they can on both feet—should be the most demanding.

Time: Any length of time desired by the coach with a 1-minute minimum for each of the first five steps. The sixth step, should be for a minimum of 2 minutes.

Coaching Points: Players must maintain balance with head up and eyes looking forward.

STEAL-THE-BALL DRILL

Purpose: To improve quickness and reaction time.

Number of Personnel: Minimum of two players and a coach or manager.

Equipment and Facilities: One basketball, one half court with foul lane marked, and a whistle for the coach or manager.

Procedure: Set up players (P in Diagram 1.2) on each side of the foul lane with a ball directly between them. Players should have their backs to the basketball. At the whistle, each player tries to grab ball and take it to the foul line without getting tagged by the other player.

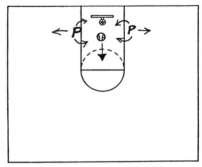

Diagram 1.2

Time: Coach determines duration.

Coaching Points: Players should maintain balance on turning in to pick up the ball and getting ball to foul line.

PASS- AND TURN-AROUND DRILL

Purpose: To improve reaction of player to where pass is thrown; to work on hands of player receiving pass and hand-eye coordination.

Number of Personnel: Minimum of two players, to work in pairs.

Equipment and Facilities: One basketball per pair.

Procedure: Coach should space two players ten to twelve feet apart. One player has a basketball and will pass it to the other player. The receiving player has back to the passing player. Player with ball passes (with either a chest pass or a bounce pass) and yells "Ball!" Receiving player turns around quickly and reacts to catch pass.

Time: Minimum of 30 seconds to maximum of 1 minute for each player.

Coaching Points: Players should follow the ball into their hands, and maintain good balance when receiving it.

REACTION DRILL

Purpose: To improve foot speed and reactions to verbal and visual stimuli.

Number of Personnel: Any number of players and a coach or squad leader.

Equipment and Facilities: No special equipment or facilities needed.

Procedure: The entire team spreads out on a half court facing the coach (see Diagram 1.3). The coach uses both visual and verbal signals so that

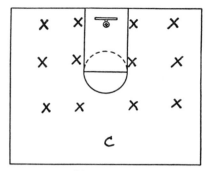

Diagram 1.3

players can react to both types of stimuli. Coach can make the following calls or signals:

(A) "Stance": Players assume a defensive stance and move their feet in a stutter step as quickly as possible.

(B) "Right": Players execute a 90° jump turn to their right and back to face coach as quickly as possible.

(C) "Left": Players do same as (B) except to their left.

(D) "180": Players execute a 180° jump back to their original position.

(E) "Up": Players stand straight up on command.

Coach could also choose to do drill with teammates following the leader imitating a player out front.

Time: Coach determines duration.

Coaching Points: Make sure that players maintain excellent defensive stance throughout drill. They should keep knees flexed and head and eyes up and looking forward.

BALL REACTION DRILL

Purpose: To improve hand reaction time and hand-eye coordination.

Number of Personnel: Minimum of two players to any number of pairs.

Equipment and Facilities: One basketball per pair.

Procedure: One player holds basketball at about chest level and then drops it. The other player takes a defensive stance approximately an arm's length from the first player, with hands behind back. The defensive player must catch the ball before it hits the ground. This drill can be varied by having the ball dropper gradually move the ball down to the stomach, hips, etc., and still have the player not bend their knees to cheat.

Coaching Points: Players should maintain balance and change partners so that they are not in the same pairs each day.

AGILITY DRILL #7

Purpose: To improve foot speed and balance.

Number of Personnel: Any number of players may perform the drill as long as the coach makes the necessary preparations. A coach or manager should be present to time the drill.

Equipment and Facilities: The area used will depend upon the number of players executing the drill. Either tape or chalk to mark the floor, a stopwatch, and a whistle will be needed.

Procedure: The coach marks the floor as shown in Diagram 1.4. The dots that make up the square should be a little more than shoulder-width apart.

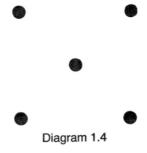

Diagram 1.4

Player begins by placing a foot on each of two corner dots. At the whistle player moves feet as quickly as possible to bring them together on the middle dot and then spreads feet again to touch the other two corner dots. Player continues the process of spreading feet and bringing them together.

Time: Coach should establish a 30- to 60-second time limit.

Coaching Points: Balance is very important. Head and eyes up and forward.

AGILITY DRILL #8

Purpose: To improve foot speed, balance, and endurance.

Number of Personnel: Any number of players can perform the drill as long as coach makes the necessary preparations. A coach or manager should keep time.

Equipment and Facilities: The amount of space needed will depend on how many players participate. Also needed: chalk or a tape to mark the floor, a whistle, and a stopwatch.

Procedure: The coach should set up the marks as shown in Diagram 1.5. The dots should be about shoulder-width apart. Players begin by standing with both feet together on one of the end dots on the line of three (A). On the whistle the players will jump with both feet together and proceed through the dot pattern, moving as quickly as possible.

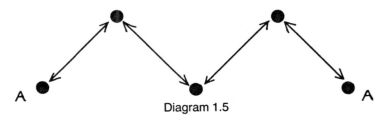

Diagram 1.5

Time: Coach will set a 30- to 60-second time limit.

Coaching Points: Balance is very important. Head and eyes up and forward.

AGILITY DRILL #9

Purpose: To improve their foot speed, balance, and endurance.

Number of Personnel: Any number of players can perform the drill as long as the coach makes the appropriate preparations. A coach or manager should keep time.

Equipment and Facilities: Chalk or tape to mark the floor, a stopwatch, and a whistle. The amount of space to be used will depend upon the number of participating players.

Procedure: Coach sets up marks on floor as shown in Diagram 1.6. The dots should be about shoulder-width apart. Player begins the drill by standing on one dot with both feet together. At the whistle the player will jump from

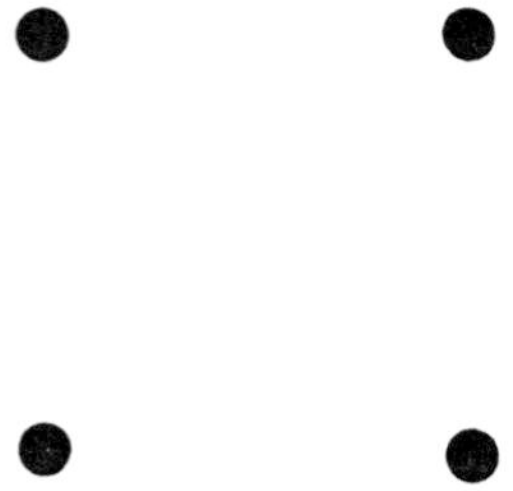

●   ●

●   ●

Diagram 1.6

dot to dot, keeping both feet together at all times. After a designated time the player should change jump direction from clockwise to counterclockwise or vice versa. Player must move as quickly as possible.

Time: Drill should run a minimum of 60 seconds with the player changing directions at the 30-second mark.

Coaching Points: Balance is very important. Head and eyes up and forward.

AGILITY DRILL #10

Purpose: To improve foot speed, balance, and endurance.

Number of Personnel: Any number of players may do the drill as long as the coach has made the necessary preparations. A coach or manager should keep time.

Equipment and Facilities: The amount of space that will be needed to do the drill will depend on the number of participating players. Also needed: a whistle, a stopwatch, and either tape or chalk to mark the floor.

Procedure: The coach draws the marks on the floor as shown in Diagram 1.7. This time the dots should not be more than six to ten inches apart. At

● ●

● ●

Diagram 1.7

the whistle players jump with both feet together and touch each dot in the small square. They continue the process for a designated amount of time and then reverse the direction of their jump from clockwise to counterclockwise or vice versa. Players must move feet as quickly as possible.

Time: A minimum of 60 seconds with players changing direction at the 30-second mark.

Coaching Points: Balance is very important. Head and eyes up and forward.

CONDITIONING DRILLS

THIRTY-SECOND LINE DRILL

Purpose: To condition and build up sprint endurance.

Number of Personnel: Any number of players that can line up across a baseline.

Equipment and Facilities: One full court and a stopwatch.

Procedure: Players start lined up on one baseline. They then run to four lines—foul line extended, half-court line, other foul line extended, and other baseline—on the court and back each time (see Diagram 2.1). Players must touch each line. Coach can have them touch line either with a foot or a hand.

Time: Players must finish one complete cycle in 30 seconds. The coach may want players to run the drill twice in a 62-second time period.

Coaching Points: Excellent for negative reinforcement and losers in competitive drills. Run with head and eyes up and under control.

TEN-SECOND DRILL

Purpose: For conditioning in sprint conditions.

Number of Personnel: Any number of players that can line up along a baseline.

Equipment and Facilities: One full court and a stopwatch.

Procedure: Players start at one baseline, run to opposite baseline, and return to starting point as quickly as possible.

Time: Must complete cycle in 10 seconds.

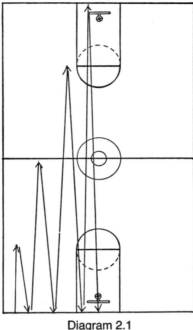

Diagram 2.1

Coaching Points: Excellent for negative reinforcement and losers in competitive drills. Run with head and eyes up and under control.

LAPS (CONDITIONING DRILL)

Purpose: To improve endurance.

Number of Personnel: Any number of players.

Equipment and Facilities: A court or large area to run and a stopwatch.

Procedure: Players run a desired number of laps around the court or area designated by the coach. Drill may be used at the beginning of practice as players jog to loosen up. Coach may also use drill as a conditioning routine or for negative reinforcement. If the drill is done for either of those two purposes, then coach must make sure to set a time limit for a desired number of laps.

Time: Coach determines duration.

Coaching Points: As a conditioning routine or for negative reinforcement. Time limit can be used on number of laps to run. Run with head and eyes up and under control.

FULL-COURT SHUFFLE

Purpose: Drill is designed to increase endurance through continuous stressful physical activity for a given time period. Players also improve their defensive stance and foot movement. The drill may also be used for negative reinforcement.

Number of Personnel: Any number of players and a coach.

Equipment and Facilities: A full court, a whistle, and a stopwatch.

Procedure: Players line up around the sidelines and baselines of a full court, facing in toward the center jump circle. At the whistle, the players assume good defensive stance and begin to shuffle counterclockwise around the full court. Every time the coach blows the whistle, players change direction. The coach must remember the following points:

1. Players *must* stay low and not straighten up, no matter how long the drill lasts.

2. Players are *not* to cross their feet or let them touch while shuffling.

3. The coach must constantly encourage players to work hard and give maximum effort for the duration of the drill.

Time: The coach establishes the time limit for the drill. It is suggested that the drill continue for a minimum of 2 minutes to a maximum of 6.

Coaching Points: Players must maintain defensive stance and keep knees flexed. Do not let players cross feet. Encourage players to work hard and maintain stance.

SEVENTEEN DRILL

Purpose: To improve conditioning in a sprint situation.

Number of Personnel: Any number.

Equipment and Facilities: One half court or full court and a stopwatch.

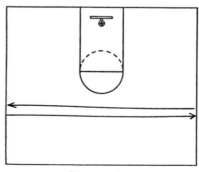

Diagram 2.2

Procedure: Players start at one sideline and run and touch the other sideline (see Diagram 2.2). They repeat the process until they have touched the sidelines a total of seventeen times.

Time: Cycle must be completed in 60 seconds.

Coaching Points: Conditioning routine or for negative reinforcement. Players must have head and eyes up and run under control.

JUMPING DRILLS

HIGH-JUMP DRILL

Purpose: To improve jumping ability; and conditioning.

Number of Personnel: Any number of players that can comfortably do drill. It will be dependent upon the number of bars or benches available for use. A coach should supervise the drill.

Equipment and Facilities: A bar or bars set up at a desired height (could be a bench or benches); perhaps a stopwatch.   Rope

Procedure: From a standing position, players jump back and forth over a bar set at a height desired by coach.

Time: The coach may either set a time limit for the drill or end drill when players have jumped across bar a given number of times.

Coaching Points: Players should maintain balance and be ready to repeat jumps.

STANDSTILL SQUATS

Purpose: To increase leg strength in order to improve jumping ability.

Number of Personnel: Any number of players and a coach.

Equipment and Facilities: No special equipment or facilities needed.

Procedure: Players begin drill by holding squat position, keeping buttocks above feet. On four counts, directed by the coach, players *gradually* rise until fully extended on their toes. They are to keep their hands in the air at all times. Coach should have players do a set of three.

Time: The four-count period of time is determined by the coach.

Coaching Points: Players must maintain balance and keep head and eyes forward.

SQUAT JUMPS TO HALF-COURT
AND BACK

Purpose: To increase leg strength in order to increase jumping ability.

Number of Personnel: Any number of players who can stand along a baseline.

Equipment and Facilities: At least a half court of space.

Procedure: Players should not bring their buttocks too low when they move into the squat position. This will help them to take it easy on their knees. Players try to jump from the squat position to half court and back in as few squat jumps as possible.

Time: Any number of times desired by the coach.

Coaching Points: Players must maintain balance and keep head and eyes up and forward.

RIM TOUCHES

Purpose: To improve jumping ability and timing for rebounding.

Number of Personnel: Depends on number of baskets available; coach should probably not use more than four players at a basket.

Equipment and Facilities: Baskets. The more baskets available, the more people the coach can work out in the drill.

Procedure: Players touch their designated target first with the right hand, then with the left hand, and then with both hands. They repeat this sequence for the duration of the drill. Players must touch rim, backboard, or spot on net ten times in a row without resting, and do a minimum of three sets. Coach could also decide to establish a time limit.

Time: Depends on the number of sets desired by coach and how many players are at a basket.

Coaching Points: Players must maintain balance, repeat jumps quickly, and get as high as possible on each jump.

TEAM JUMP ROPE

Purpose: To condition and increase leg strength in order to improve jumping ability.

Number of Personnel: As many players as can fit comfortably alongside the ropes, and a coach.

Equipment and Facilities: Three twenty-foot-long ropes tied to a height of about one foot; a stopwatch.

Procedure: Coach should divide team among the three ropes. All players start on the same side of the rope. On command, the players jump back and forth over the rope without touching it.

Time: Should start doing drill for a 3-minute time period and gradually increase to 5 or 6 minutes.

Coaching Points: Players must maintain balance and be ready to repeat jumps, head and eyes up.

JUMPING ABILITY DRILL

Purpose: To improve leg strength in order to increase jumping ability.

Number of Personnel: Any number of players and a coach or manager.

Equipment and Facilities: Possibly a stopwatch.

Procedure: Players should jump as high as they can, using a "scissors" action with their legs each time they jump.

Time: Either repeat drill twenty-five times or for a given period desired by the coach. Number of sets to be determined by the coach.

Coaching Points: When landing, players should be on balance and ready to repeat jumps.

ADDITIONAL JUMPING ABILITY DRILL

Purpose: To improve leg strength in order to increase jumping ability.

Number of Personnel: Any number of players and a coach.

Equipment and Facilities: Possibly a stopwatch.

Procedure: Players place hands on shoulders, so as to offer resistance to their jumping and jump as high as they can.

Time: May either repeat drill twenty-five times or for a given period desired by the coach. Number of sets to be determined by the coach.

Coaching Points: When landing, players should be on balance and ready to repeat jump.

BALL HANDLING DRILLS

UCLA SERIES

(Done length of the court. Set up four lines per court along one of the baselines.)

Purpose: To teach and improve proper footwork needed in offensive and defensive skills; to improve player's ability to execute the basic types of dribbles.

Number of Personnel: One to twenty-four players and a coach.

Equipment and Facilities: One full court and at least four basketballs.

Procedure: The drill consists of the eleven maneuvers described below.

1. *Change of Direction Cut.* All players begin by taking three steps to the right. They plant the foot in the direction they are moving (in this case the right foot). They now must make a good "V" cut by picking up the other foot (in this case the left foot) and sending it in the opposite direction. Now they continue to the left and repeat the process (plant left foot and send right one in opposite direction). Players should continue the process up and back down the court. (Do not use a ball.)

2. *Stop-Starts.* Players start running at full speed. When they reach the foul line they slow almost to a complete stop. They then accelerate back to full speed and then repeat the process when they reach the half-court line, going the full length of the court and back, slowing at each foul line and the half-court line. (Do not use a ball.)

3. *Hockey-Step.* Players will do the same process as in (2) but this time when slowing down they bang their feet as quickly as possible. (Do not use a ball.)

4. *Defensive Change of Direction.* Players assume a defensive stance on a baseline facing out of bounds. All players begin by going to the right. They

shuffle to the right for three steps. They then plant the foot in the direction they are going (in this case the right foot) and use it as a pivot foot. They then swing the left leg and foot to open up. Now players shuffle to the left and repeat process (plant left foot, use it as a pivot foot, and open up the right leg and foot). Continue process up and back down the length of the court. (Do not use a ball.)

5. *Offensive and Defensive Change of Direction.* Coach puts two players together as partners, one on offense and the other on defense. They do drills (1) and (4). When they go the length of the court, they switch assignments and come back down the court. (Do not use a ball.)

6. *Offensive Change of Direction.* This time players use a basketball, working on the crossover dribble. The footwork is the same as in (1). In dribbling, players use the right hand when moving to the right and the left hand when going left. They make the crossover dribble when they make their "V" cut. They should make sure they keep the ball low when changing hands.

7. *Hockey-Step Dribble.* Same drill as in (3) except that players use a ball for dribbling practice. They make sure to keep control of the basketball while doing the hockey step, dribbling with the right hand going up the court and with the left hand coming back down.

8. *Stop-and-Go Dribble.* Same drill as in (2) except that, again, players use a ball for dribbling practice. Coach must make sure players push the ball out in front of them when they move at full speed and keep basketball under control when slowing down. Players use only the right hand going up the court and only the left hand coming back down.

9. *Offensive Back Down Court Dribble.* The foot movement is the same as in Drill (4); the only difference is that the players back the ball down the court. Players must keep their bodies between the defensive player and the ball. When they move left, they should: (1) look over the left shoulder; (2) keep left arm up to ward off defensive player; and (3) dribble with the right hand. When they move right, they simply reverse the motions: (1) look over right shoulder; (2) right arm up; (3) dribble with left hand. They do this all the way up the court and then back down.

10. *Spin Dribble.* Players dribble with right hand, moving straight toward other baseline. After approximately three steps players will plant opposite foot (left foot) and swing the other foot behind the planted foot (in this case they swing the right foot behind the left). Players pull basketball around in one dribble with the same hand (in this case the right hand) a complete 180°. Once ball has gone the 180°, then players dribble with the left hand. Now, they dribble with the left hand, plant the right foot, swing left foot behind, etc. Process should be repeated all the way up and back down the court.

11. *Speed Dribble.* Players try to dribble as quickly as possible, pushing

the ball out in front of them. They should go up the court with the right hand and come back using only the left hand.

Time: Do the entire drill series. Time will depend on the number of players doing the drill.

Coaching Points: See Appendix A–I, Ball Handling.

DRIBBLE SERIES

Purpose: To improve skill in the four basic dribbles with both hands and execution of right- and left-hand lay-ups.

Number of Personnel: One to ten players per half court.

Equipment and Facilities: One full court and at least four basketballs.

Procedure: Players work on the four basic dribbles: speed, change-of-pace, crossover, and spin. Starting at point A (see Diagram 4.1), they execute speed dribble with the right hand and make the lay-up. They then dribble the ball out to point B with the left hand and again execute the speed dribble and make the lay-up. Players now dribble back out to point A with the right hand and then execute second dribble with right hand and make a lay-up. Players continue process until they have completed all four dribbles.

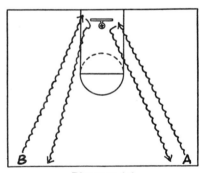

Diagram 4.1

Time: At least one completion of the series. Time will depend on the number of players on a half court.

Coaching Points: See Appendix A–I, Ball Handling; Appendix A–II, Shooting.

WHISTLE BALL-HANDLING DRILL

Purpose: To improve speed dribble, control and protect the basketball while dribbling.

Number of Personnel: Four to twenty-four players, depending on the number of basketballs that are available, and a coach.

Equipment and Facilities: At least four basketballs, preferably more. A whistle for use by the coach.

Procedure: Players line up on a baseline, facing the coach (see Diagram 4.2). Each player should have a ball. At the first whistle players speed dribble toward the coach. At second whistle players stop and control basketball. Coach may come by a player and try to steal the ball. Players must protect the basketball. At the next whistle, they speed dribble again, and the process is repeated.

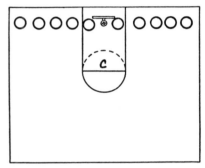

Diagram 4.2

Time: 3 to 5 minutes or whatever time is desired by the coach.

Coaching Points: See Appendix A–I, Ball Handling.

LINE-DRIBBLING DRILL

Purpose: Dribble practice.

Number of Personnel: One to fifteen players and a coach.

Equipment and Facilities: At least four basketballs but, ideally, one per player. Also need one full court.

Procedure: At Position 1 (see Diagram 4.3) players execute a fingertip control dribble until coach signals first player to begin. Wherever there is a 2 on the diagram, players execute a spin dribble. Other types of dribbles that are included in the drill and listed on the diagram are:

(3) Behind the back

(4) Crossover

(5) Hockey Step

(6) Hesitation—Stop and Go

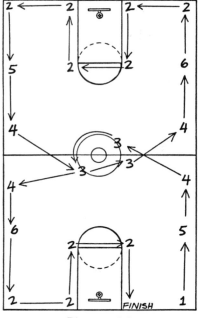

Diagram 4.3

Time: All players should complete at least one full trip; time will depend on the number of players involved in the drill.

Coaching Points: See Appendix A–I, Ball Handling.

DRIBBLE TAG

Purpose: To work on basketball control while moving quickly.

Number of Personnel: Four to eighteen players and coach.

Equipment and Facilities: A basketball per player and a half court.

Procedure: Players are restricted to a half-court area. Two players are "it" and must hold one hand up until they tag another player. Any player who loses control of the ball while making a tag is still "it." Players continue to dribble and stay in the designated area. The drill can be performed by having all players use just their weak hand or just their strong hand. Coach may have them use strong and/or weak hand.

Time: Drill runs for 2 to 5 minutes. At the end of the time period, the two players who are "it" and any players who did not continuously dribble the ball or stay in the designated area must run a 30-second line drill.

Coaching Points: See Appendix A–I, Ball Handling.

TWO-AGAINST-EIGHT DRILL

Purpose: To teach players to handle pressure while bringing the ball up-court.

Number of Personnel: Minimum of ten players to a maximum of twenty.

Equipment and Facilities: At least one basketball and a full court.

Procedure: Players 1 and 2 (see Diagram 4.4) try to advance the ball the length of the court, from one baseline to the other. The two defensive players in each of the designated areas try to steal the ball. The Xs play defense only in their area. The two Xs in Area 1 become the next offensive players. Players 1 and 2 become the defensive players in Area 4 while other defensive players rotate up one area.

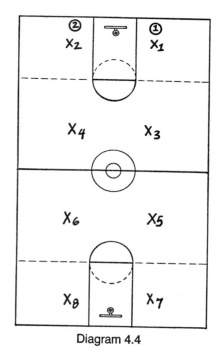

Diagram 4.4

Time: Drill continues for as long as it takes for all players to attempt drill at least once.

Coaching Points: Coach can place a limit on the number of dribbles the offensive people are allowed to use. See Appendix A–I, Ball Handling; Appendix B–I, On-the-Ball Defense: Appendix B–II, Off-the-Ball Defense.

DRIBBLE INDIVIDUAL GAME DRILL

Purpose: To teach players to protect the basketball while dribbling and make players dribble with head up.

Number of Personnel: Five to fifteen players and a coach.

Equipment and Facilities: A foul lane or a circle on the basketball court and five basketballs.

Procedure: Drill begins with five players in a circle at the foul lane, each with a basketball. Each player tries to knock the ball away from another and out of the circle. When the ball goes out of the circle, then that player is out of the game. Players continue to dribble until they are eliminated. The last player left "wins."

Time: Drill continues until there is only one player left in the circle. The other four players should run a 30-second drill. Length of drill will depend on the skills of the players involved and how many players are to execute the drill.

Coaching Points: See Appendix A–I, Ball Handling.

TWO-BALL RELAY DRILL

Purpose: To teach players to dribble with either hand to develop agility.

Number of Personnel: Two to twenty players and a coach.

Equipment and Facilities: Four basketballs and a full court. Can be done with four or five squads, with two basketballs per squad.

Procedure: The team divides into two competing squads. The coach will station half of each squad on each baseline. Each player at the front of the line dribbles to the opposite baseline with two balls. A player who loses control of either ball must go back to the starting point. The first squad finished wins. The coach could also elect to do same relay type of situation with only one ball for each squad and designate whether it should be a strong-hand or off-hand dribble.

Time: Drill continues until one of the two squads wins.

Coaching Points: Emphasize to players the need to try to keep their heads up at all times. See Appendix A–I, Ball Handling.

STATIONARY BALL DRILLS

Purpose: Familiarity with ball handling, quickness, and agility.

Number of Personnel: Any number of players.

Equipment and Facilities: A basketball for each player.

Procedure:

1. *Bounce and Catch*. Player spreads legs and bounces ball hard through legs and catches it by moving hands behind back. Player then throws ball from back to front, continuing process for 30 to 45 seconds.

2. *Walking*. Player crouches down and walks forward, moving ball between legs from one hand to the other with each step. Player tries to increase speed.

3. *Around One Leg*. Player spreads legs and moves ball around one leg as quickly as possible. After a period of time, reverse the direction. When finished with the one leg, player then does the same drill around the other leg. Drill lasts 30 seconds for each leg.

4. *Around Both Legs*. Player puts feet together and moves ball around legs as quickly as possible for 30 to 45 seconds, then reverses direction for the same amount of time.

5. *Around the Waist*. Player places the ball in either hand and takes it behind the lower back, catches it with the other hand, and in one continuous motion brings the ball around to the front. The process should go as quickly as possible. Player does the drill for 30 seconds and repeats by moving the ball in the opposite direction.

6. *Around the Head*. Player places ball in either hand, and with shoulders back takes the ball behind the head, catches it with the opposite hand, and brings it around to the front. Repeat the process with a continuous motion for 30 seconds and then repeat the process by moving the ball in the opposite direction.

7. *Head, Waist, and Leg Drill*. Player starts with ball in either hand and takes it around the head to the other hand. In one continuous motion, the player then takes the ball around the waist and down around the legs. From the legs, player goes up around the waist to up around the head again. Player should try to move the basketball as quickly as possible. Repeat the process moving the ball in the opposite direction.

8. *One-Hand Bounce Between Legs*. Player uses only one hand to control the ball. Starting with the ball in front, in either hand, player takes the ball around one leg and bounces it once between the legs. The player then catches it in front of body with the same hand. Repeat process as quickly as possible. Player then follows the same routine with the other hand.

9. *Two Balls Through the Legs*. Player begins with a ball in each hand, takes the balls behind legs and at the same time bounces them between legs. As soon as they bounce once the player must bring hands back to the front and catch both balls with right and left hands. Player continues executing the same motion for a given period of time, doing the drill as quickly as possible.

10. *Two Ball Alternating Drill.* Player should have a ball in each hand and begin the drill by taking the right-hand ball behind legs and bouncing it between them, bringing the right hand to the front to catch it. As player is about to catch the ball with the right hand, he or she takes the left-hand ball behind the legs and bounces it between them just as before. Player should continue drill alternating the two balls. There should be no time limit on this drill. It will be difficult at first; the player will need to spend less time on the drill after becoming more proficient.

11. *Double Leg, Single Leg.* With both legs together, player starts with a ball in the right hand and takes it behind the legs and around to the front via the left hand. When the ball reaches the right hand in front, the player spreads legs and takes the ball around the right leg using both hands. Player then closes legs and takes the ball once around both legs, then opens legs and takes the ball around left leg once, then back to two legs again. The ball always moves in the same direction. Player does this for 30 seconds. Player should repeat drill, moving the ball in the opposite direction.

12. *Figure Eight.* Player begins with the ball in either hand in back of legs, then takes it between legs to the other hand. He or she now takes the ball behind leg and between the legs to the hand with which player began the drill. Player should continue the process as quickly as possible, never allowing ball to touch the floor. Player then repeats the process, moving the figure eight in the opposite direction.

13. *Figure Eight Dribble.* Player starts by doing the same as the figure eight drill, but dribbling the basketball as well, keeping the ball as low as possible at all times. Player should do drill as quickly as possible without losing control of the ball.

14. *Two-Bounce Drill.* Player starts with ball in either hand, and proceeds as in the figure eight drill except that each time he or she takes the ball through the legs, it must be bounced from one hand to the other. The faster the player gets at performing the drill, the lower the ball will be.

15. *Figure Eight with One Bounce.* Player continues as in the figure eight drill, but upon completing each figure eight drops the ball between the legs. Player should do drill as quickly as possible.

16. *Spider Drill.* Player begins in a crouched position, holding a ball in front of body. Now, with legs apart, he or she takes one dribble with either hand and one dribble with opposite hand. On the second dribble the player takes the first hand behind legs and dribbles once, immediately bringing the opposite hand behind the legs to dribble once. Then the player goes back to the front and so on. There should be two bounces in the front and two behind, with the ball as close to the floor as possible.

17. *Quick Hands Drill.* Player starts with ball between legs, which are about shoulder-width apart. One hand is on ball in front of legs and the other hand

on the ball in the back of the legs. Player flips the ball in the air and reverses the position of the hands, catching the ball with fingertips. The ball should not hit the floor.

18. *Flip.* Drill begins with player's legs shoulder-width apart, knees bent, and hands in front holding the basketball. The ball is released or flipped very slightly up in the air between legs. Player now brings hands to the back of legs and catches ball before it hits the ground. The player again flips ball in the air and brings hands to the front of the body as quickly as possible. Player should do the drill as fast as possible without dropping the ball.

Time: Each drill lasts 30 to 60 seconds. The coach may have players perform one or all eighteen of the drills.

Coaching Points: Coach must be aware that certain of these details are progressive. Thoroughly check drills before selecting. See Appendix A–I, Ball Handling.

PICK-UP DRILL

Purpose: To teach offensive players to protect the ball and keep it from getting stolen. To teach defensive players to be quick and slap ball away from offensive player.

Number of Personnel: A minimum of five players to a maximum of fifteen and a coach.

Equipment and Facilities: Four basketballs, a half court, and a stopwatch.

Procedure: Coach places five players on a baseline and four basketballs on the nearest foul line (see Diagram 4.5). At the whistle or on command the players run to get a ball. The player without a ball must try to steal one from another player. The other four players must stay in the front court. Coach runs the drill for one minute. At the end of one minute, the player without a ball runs three 10-second drills. The drill is repeated with four players and

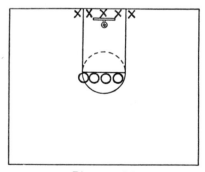

Diagram 4.5

three basketballs. The losers run two 10-second drills. The drill continues until there are only two players and one basketball. The loser of that last competition runs only one 10-second drill. The coach should call fouls which force a player to lose the basketball.

Time: To complete the entire cycle of the drill, it will take approximately 5 minutes.

Coaching Points: See Appendix A–I, Ball Handling; Appendix B–I, On-the-Ball Defense.

TWO-ON-ONE DRILL

Purpose: For players to learn to advance the basketball up-court under extreme pressure.

Number of Personnel: Nine to eighteen players in groups of three.

Equipment and Facilities: A full court and three basketballs.

Procedure: The court is divided into three separate lanes with an offensive player with a basketball and two defensive players in each lane (see Diagram 4.6). Coach should match up guards with guards, forwards with forwards, and centers with centers. Offensive players dribble basketball the length of

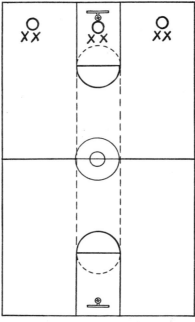

Diagram 4.6

the court against the two defensive players. Offense must stay in their lane. When players reach the end of the court, they change roles. Thus an offensive player changes to defense, and vice versa. Drill should be repeated as many times as desired by the coach, who makes sure that each player handles the ball at least once.

Time: Time depends on the number of players and their level of skill.

Coaching Points: See Appendix A–I, Ball Handling; Appendix B–I, On-the-Ball Defense.

POUND BALL

Purpose: To accustom players to having a basketball thrust upon them with force.

Number of Personnel: Any number of players.

Equipment and Facilities: A basketball for each player.

Procedure: Player should pound ball as hard as possible from one hand to the other, quickly and authoritatively. Player can do this drill any time during the day.

Time: The basketball should touch each hand a minimum of twenty-five times.

Coaching Points: See Appendix A–I, Ball Handling.

DRIBBLING DRILL

Purpose: For players to learn to execute five types of dribbles.

Number of Personnel: One to eighteen players.

Equipment and Facilities: As many basketballs as possible (ideally one per player) and a half court.

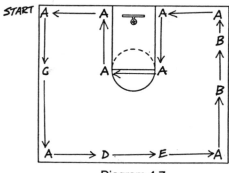

Diagram 4.7

Procedure: Players do the following dribbles at each of the points indicated in Diagram 4.7:

(A) spin dribble

(B) crossover dribble

(C) speed dribble

(D) change-of-pace dribble

(E) hockey step dribble

Time: Drill can be completed either a desired number of times or for a set period desired by the coach.

Coaching Points: See Appendix A–I, Ball Handling.

DEFENSIVE DRILLS

NORTH CAROLINA ZIGZAG SERIES

Purpose: To improve defensive footwork and foot speed. Players learn to stay low and to play defense against a player with the basketball. They also learn to turn the offensive player and open up in order to continue to guard aggressively the player with the ball. An excellent conditioning drill.

Number of Personnel: Any number of players (from two to twenty-six) and a coach.

Equipment and Facilities: Need a full court and at least six basketballs.

Procedure:

1. *Defensive Movement.* Players start in defensive stance, with no ball, at the corner of a baseline and shuffle towards the foul lane (see Diagram 5.1). When players reach the foul-lane line they plant their foot nearest the foul lane and open up with the other leg and shuffle toward the sideline. Players keep their head up and eyes forward, staying down in the stance, and do not cross their feet or let their feet touch. They continue the process to the other baseline, then sprint across baseline and repeat process going back down court.

2. *Offensive and Defensive Movement.* Players now use a ball. They do the same as in (1) except that the coach adds an offensive player dribbling the basketball. Offensive players do not try to beat the defensive players but are supposed to make them work. Defensive players do not try to steal ball but try to beat the offensive player to the sideline and foul lane line each time. Players should switch assignments when they reach the end of the court. Coach may wish to insert an additional step in the drill. Process is the same as (2) only without the ball. This can be done between Steps (1) and (2).

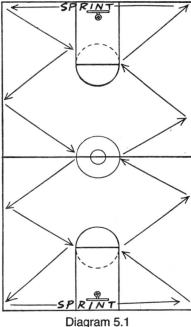

Diagram 5.1

Time: A suggested minimum of 3 minutes for each step.

Coaching Points: See Appendix B–I, On-the-Ball Defense.

DENY DRILL

Purpose: For players to be able to properly deny a pass to the wings in a player-to-player defense.

Number of Personnel: Minimum of three players to a maximum of eighteen and a coach.

Equipment and Facilities: One basketball (minimum) and a half court. Could have one group of players on each side of a half court. Would then need a minimum of two basketballs.

Procedure: Passer is on one side of the top of the key (see Diagram 5.2). Defensive player tries to deny the pass to offensive player. Offensive player may use only half the court to try to get open. Defensive player is on the right side of the court, right hand up in the passing lane and left arm up with forearm blocking offensive player and any attempts at offensive backdoor move. Defensive player makes the offensive player run into the forearm in order to slow down the backdoor move. If offensive player gains possession of ball, then the pair plays one-on-one on that half of the court. When offensive

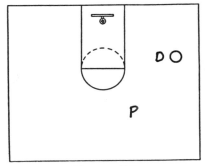

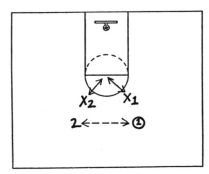

Diagram 5.2   Diagram 5.3

player is on left side of the court, then defensive player should have left hand in the passing lane and right forearm up, and so on. Coach should make sure to do drill on both sides of the court. The coach could rotate players or run them through in pairs.

Time: A minimum of 5 minutes to a maximum of 15 minutes.

Coaching Points: See Appendix B–II, Off-the-Ball Defense.

OFF- AND TO-THE-BALL DRILL

Purpose: Proper positioning of guards on a guard-to-guard pass in player-to-player defense.

Number of Personnel: Minimum of four players to a maximum of sixteen and a coach.

Equipment and Facilities: One basketball and a half court.

Procedure: Offensive players pass the ball back and forth. Defensive players work on going off the player they are guarding and towards the ball when their player passes the ball. Players should work together in pairs (see Diagram 5.3).

Time: Any amount of time the coach desires. It will usually depend upon number of participating personnel.

Coaching Points: See Appendix B–II, Off-the-Ball Defense.

DRIBBLE PICK-UP DRILL

Purpose: To play aggressively against the player who picks up the dribble. Also, to work on hand and arm reaction to take away passing lanes.

Number of Personnel: A minimum of two to a maximum of eighteen and a coach. Players should run through drill in pairs.

Equipment and Facilities: One basketball (minimum) and a half court.

Procedure: The offensive player dribbles toward the coach. Coach yells "Pick it up" after the offensive player has taken several dribbles. The defensive player tightly guards the offensive player to prevent a pass to the coach (see Diagram 5.4).

Time: Any amount of time desired by the coach. Again, will depend on number of participating players.

Coaching Points: Coach must encourage defensive player to be aggressive and prevent pass. See Appendix B–I.

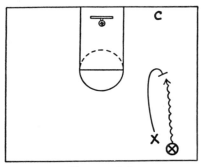

Diagram 5.4

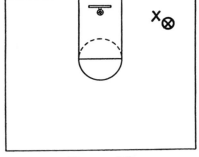

Diagram 5.5

NO BASELINE DRILL

Purpose: Work on player-to-player defense; prevent offensive player from driving the baseline; working on defensive player's on-the-ball defense and boxing out after shot.

Number of Personnel: Minimum of two to a maximum of eighteen players and a coach.

Equipment and Facilities: Minimum of one basketball and a half court.

Procedure: Drill is designed to work on the forward position along the baseline. Defensive player must make baseline foot the "up" foot in the defensive stance, and should also guard the offensive player a half-player ahead in order to take away the baseline. Defense attempts to prevent offense from driving the baseline, playing one-on-one defense and concentrating on boxing out after the shot. After completing drill on one side of the floor players will execute the drill from the other side of the floor (see Diagram 5.5).

Time: Time to be determined by coach and the number of participating players.

Coaching Points: See Appendix B–I, On-the-Ball Defense.

REBOUND-AND-REACT DRILL

Purpose: Offense: improving (1) the shot, and (2) offensive outside moves. Defense: improving (1) rebounding and outlet skills, (2) ability to react to an offensive player receiving a pass, and (3) on-the-ball defense.

Number of Personnel: Minimum of two to a maximum of eighteen and a coach.

Equipment and Facilities: Minimum of one basketball and a half court.

Procedure: Player 1 shoots the basketball. Player X1 rebounds the shot and then throws the ball back out to the offensive player and proceeds to play one-on-one. Coach must make sure that players work on both sides of the court (see Diagram 5.6).

Time: A minimum of 5 minutes to a maximum of 15 minutes.

Coaching Points: See Appendix B–I, On-the-Ball Defense; Appendix B–III, Defensive Rebounding; Appendix A–II, Shooting; Appendix A–VI, Outside Moves.

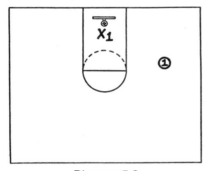
Diagram 5.6

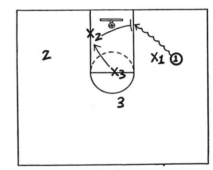
Diagram 5.7

WEAK-SIDE FORWARD DRILL

Purpose: Emphasis on defensive help-and-recover work. Weak-side forward steps in to stop penetration of offensive player to the basket and then recovering to guard own player. Defensive guard practices dropping down to ball line to give help.

Number of Personnel: Minimum of six to a maximum of eighteen players and a coach.

Equipment and Facilities: One basketball and a half court.

Procedure: Player 1 (see Diagram 5.7) drives the baseline so that Player X2 can give help to teammate. The guard (X3) drops as far as the ball goes in order to help out. Player X1 must stay with player who has driven baseline. X2 helps X1 and then recovers to own player.

Time: Time depends upon the coach's desires, but there should be a maximum of 15 minutes.

Coaching Points: See Appendix B–II, Off-the-Ball Defense.

DEFENDING THE FLASH PIVOT

Purpose: For players to learn the defensive fundamentals of defending a flash pivot into the lane.

Number of Personnel: Minimum of four players and a coach.

Equipment and Facilities: A half court and at least one basketball.

Procedure 1: On the first step made toward baseline by Player 2, Player X2 drops baseline foot (see Diagram 5.8). Then 2 moves to the high post. On the defensive slide up, X2 uses hand in the passing lane to deny pass to offensive player.

Procedure 2: Procedure is the same as previous drill but, after coming up to high post Player 2 cuts backdoor. Coach should have X2 open up and make contact with offensive player on backdoor move to prevent pass (see Diagram 5.9).

Time: Drills should be run for 5 to 10 minutes each, depending on number of participating players.

Coaching Points: See Appendix B–II, Off-the-Ball Defense.

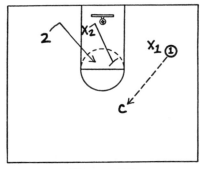

Diagram 5.8

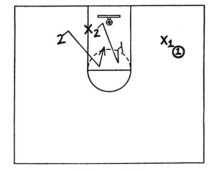

Diagram 5.9

DEFENDING FLASH PIVOT
AND REACT DRILL

Purpose: Defensive techniques against a flash pivot into the lane and reaction to cover an immediate scoring threat.

Number of Personnel: Minimum of three players and a coach.

Equipment and Facilities: A half court and a minimum of one basketball.

Procedure: Player 2 flash pivots into high post to begin the drill (see Diagram 5.10). Player X2 guards using proper defensive techniques against the flash pivot. Player 2 recovers and passes to 3. Defensive player works on quick reaction to a scoring threat. The coach can also throw to 2 to keep up X2's defensive awareness.

Time: 3 to 10 minutes, depending on the number of players involved.

Coaching Points: See Appendix B–II, Off-the-Ball Defense.

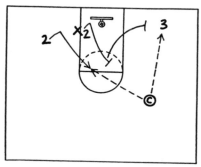

Diagram 5.10

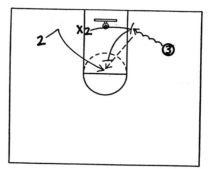

Diagram 5.11

HELP-AND-RECOVER DRILL
(FROM SIDE)

Purpose: To teach defensive players to block an immediate scoring attempt from the side and then react to any pass to the offensive player they are guarding.

Number of Personnel: Minimum of three players and a coach.

Equipment and Facilities: A half court and at least one basketball.

Procedure: Player 3 dribbles the ball along the baseline looking to score on drive (see Diagram 5.11). X2 helps out defense to prevent score. Player 3 passes to 2 in the flash pivot. X2 must react quickly to player 2 in a one-on-one situation.

Time: 3 to 10 minutes, depending on the number of participating players.

Coaching Points: See Appendix B–II, Off-the-Ball Defense; Appendix B–I, On-the-Ball Defense.

DEFENDING-THE-POST DRILL

Purpose: Defense: continually fronting offensive post players and teaching the defensive post player to react quickly to where the ball is passed on the perimeter. Offense post player works on posting-up techniques and inside moves once he or she receives a pass.

Number of Personnel: Minimum of five players and a coach.

Equipment and Facilities: A half court and a minimum of one basketball.

Procedure: The three perimeter players pass the ball around, trying to get it to the offensive post player (see Diagram 5.12). They may not throw a lob pass into the post. The offensive low post player stays stationary until the ball is passed among the perimeter players. Defensive player works on denying the pass into the post by maintaining a fronting position and reacting quickly to where the ball is passed on the perimeter. The coach should set up players in the post according to height and position so that there are no gross mismatches.

Time: From 5 to 10 minutes. Each defensive player should be able to maintain proper post defense for a minimum of 30 seconds.

Coaching Points: See Appendix B–II, Off-the-Ball Defense.

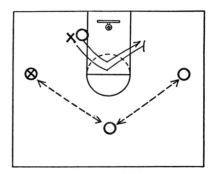

Diagram 5.12

DEFENDING-ON-SCREENS DRILL

Purpose: To teach how to defend against screens in the lane area. Offensive players learn to set screens and proper techniques of coming off a screen, and work on inside moves once they receive a pass.

Number of Personnel: Minimum of seven players and a coach.

Equipment and Facilities: A half court and at least one basketball.

Procedure: The three outside players (see Diagram 5.13) pass ball around the perimeter. The two inside offensive players screen for each other and move, while the two inside defensive players defend against the screens. Defensive players must use check-and-recover technique or switching, whichever the coach prefers, on screen situations. Defensive players must talk to one another and must also front the offensive players to keep ball from getting inside. The check-and-recover technique involves the defensive player on the person setting the screen, steps out to slow down the offensive player coming off the screen allowing defensive teammate time to fight over top of screen and then recovering quickly to continue to play the person being guarded originally.

Time: 5 to 10 minutes depending on number of players involved.

Coaching Points: See Appendix B–II, Off-the-Ball Defense.

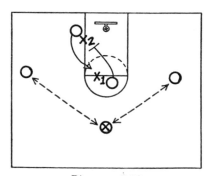

Diagram 5.13

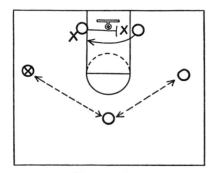

Diagram 5.14

DEFENDING-AGAINST-
THE-LOW-EXCHANGE DRILL

Purpose: Defensive low post players work on defending the low exchange while offensive post players practice proper screening techniques. Offensive perimeter players practice passing into a post player.

Number of Personnel: Minimum of seven players and a coach.

Equipment and Facilities: A half court and at least one basketball.

Procedure: The three outside players pass ball around the perimeter and the two inside offensive players work on the low-exchange screening technique (see Diagram 5.14). The two inside defensive players try to defend against the exchange. They may use the check-and-recover technique or switching technique against the low exchange. The defensive players must talk to each other and front the offensive post players to keep ball from getting inside.

Time: 5 to 10 minutes depending upon the number of participating players.

Coaching Points: See Appendix B–II, Off-the-Ball Defense.

FRONTING-THE-CUTTER
CONTINUOUS DRILL

Purpose: Defensive players learn to jump off the player they are defending and towards the ball in order to front a cutter to the basket. Offensive players practice proper give-and-go techniques.

Number of Personnel: Minimum of six players and a coach.

Equipment and Facilities: A half court and one basketball.

Procedure: The point player on offense passes to a wing and cuts for the basket (see Diagram 5.15). The defense works on fronting the cutter to the basket. The coach could put a player in the high post and have cutter cut off him or her. Defensive player defending the cutter must remember to jump off player being guarded in the direction of the pass as soon as his or her player makes the pass. Player must make cutter cut behind. For continuity, the opposite wing comes to the point and offensive cutter replaces the weak side wing.

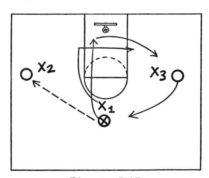

Diagram 5.15

Time: 3 to 10 minutes, depending upon the number of participating players.

Coaching Points: See Appendix B–II, Off-the-Ball Defense.

SHELL DRILL

Purpose: Teaches proper team defense according to the position of the basketball and the position of a guarded player.

Number of Personnel: Minimum of eight players and a coach.

Equipment and Facilities: A half court and one basketball.

Procedure: Start with four offensive players, two guards at the top of the key and two forwards at the mid-lane wing positions. The offensive players remain stationary at the beginning of the drill. The offense passes the ball around the perimeter. Coach could later tell offensive wings to drive the baseline if they are given the opportunity. The coach can also tell opposite wing to come across and post up when ball is in the other wing's hands. The coach could also put in guards cutting down the lane when they pass to the wing or the opposite guard without the ball down screening for the forward on their side. Defensive players try to maintain proper defensive position as ball is passed around the perimeter by the offensive players. Proper positions are shown in Diagrams 5.16A through 5.16D.

> *Diagram 5.16A:* Opposite guard (X2) is off his or her player and towards the ball, ballside forward (X4) is in deny position, and weak side forward (X3) has one foot in the lane while keeping in sight both the ball and the player he or she is guarding.

> *Diagram 5.16B:* Same as Diagram 5.16A except ball is in other guard's possession.

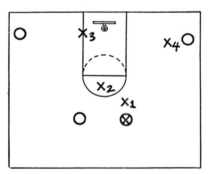

Diagram 5.16A

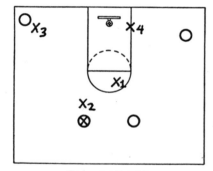

Diagram 5.16B

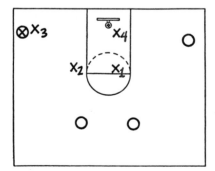

Diagram 5.16C

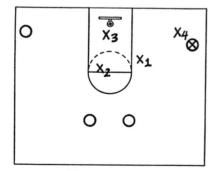

Diagram 5.16D

Diagram 5.16C: Ballside guard (X2) is off player and toward the ball, weak side guard (X1) has one foot in the lane while keeping in sight both the ball and player he or she is covering. Weak side forward (X4) has both feet in the lane without going past the basket while keeping in sight both the ball and the guarded player.

Diagram 5.16D: Same as Diagram 5.16C except ball is in the other forward's possession.

Time: 5 to 15 minutes depending upon the number of participating players and how many additional stages the coach wishes to accomplish.

Coaching Points: See Appendix B–I, On-the-Ball Defense; Appendix B–II, Off-the-Ball Defense.

ADDITION-TO-SHELL DRILL

Purpose: Defensive players learn to jump off their guarded players to pre-vent a drive to the basket and to take a charge and rotation of help against a drive to the basket from the baseline.

Number of Personnel: A minimum of ten players and a coach.

Equipment and Facilities: A half court and one basketball.

Procedure: Coach sets up the same format as in normal Shell Drill, but places an offensive player in each corner (see Diagram 5.16E). The four offensive players in the normal Shell Drill may pass to players in the corner. On receiving a pass, a corner player goes hard to the basket for a lay-up. The defensive player must make proper rotations to help stop drive. The coach should look for one of the defensive players to draw a charge.

Time: 5 to 10 minutes, depending on number of participating players involved.

Coaching Points: See Appendix B–I, On-the-Ball Defense; Appendix B–II, Off-the-Ball Defense.

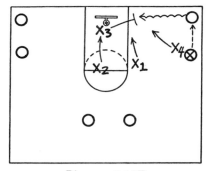

Diagram 5.16E

TWO-ON-TWO DRILL

Purpose: Defensive players practice proper techniques against any offensive moves associated with two-on-two basketball. Offensive players work at improving their one-on-one moves, pick-and-roll, and give-and-go techniques.

Number of Personnel: Minimum of four players to a maximum of twelve.

Equipment and Facilities: A half court and a basketball.

Procedure: Offensive players work on give and go and proper screen and roll techniques. The defensive players work on making cutters cut behind them, fighting over a pick, and check-and-recover or switching techniques in defending against a screen. Coach should limit the number of dribbles for the offensive players to two or three.

Time: A minimum of 5 minutes to a maximum of 10.

Coaching Points: See Appendix B–I, On-the-Ball Defense; Appendix B–II, Off-the-Ball Defense.

VAN LIER DRILL

Purpose: Emphasis on defense: players are rewarded if they prevent the opposing team from scoring.

Number of Personnel: A minimum of nine players to a maximum of fifteen; desirable to have players in groups of three. Coach to supervise.

Equipment and Facilities: A half court and one basketball.

Procedure: Coach divides the team into groups of three and puts them in an order. Objective of the drill is to play sound defense and prevent opponents from scoring. If the defensive team steals the ball, forces a turnover, or gets a rebound they become the new offensive team, and a new defensive team is called out onto the floor. If the offensive team scores, then·a new offensive team is called out on the floor. The ball must be checked by the coach after the defense comes up with the ball or if the offense scores. Teams not on the floor must be ready to come out on the floor quickly.

Time: To be decided by the coach.

Coaching Points: See Appendix B–I, On-the-Ball Defense; Appendix B–II, Off-the-Ball Defense.

ONE-ON-ONE DRILL

Purpose: Defensive player practices proper on-the-ball defense techniques while offensive player works on one-on-one moves.

Number of Personnel: A minimum of two to a maximum of ten per basket, and a coach.

Equipment and Facilities: A half court for each group of players; a basketball for each set of partners if possible.

Procedure: Offensively, players are working on good one-on-one moves (Jab Step Series, etc.). Defensively, players work on the fundamentals the coach has established for playing sound on-the-ball defense: quick foot movement, staying low and in a good defensive stance, concentrating on the belt of the offensive player, either playing straight up on the player or half-player ahead and trying to force offensive player a particular direction, arm's length distance between offensive and defensive player, defending a shot by taking a step toward the offensive player and extending both arms straight up or going straight up with shooter only when he/she leaves the floor, and so on. The coach may want to limit the number of dribbles to one, two or three. The drill should be done first with hands behind the defensive player's back. If this is done, then the offensive player can go in only one direction. After a period of time defensive player may use hands on defense.

Time: A minimum of 5 minutes to a maximum of 10.

Coaching Points: See Appendix B–I, On-the-Ball Defense; Appendix A–VI, Outside Moves.

HELP-AND-RECOVER DRILL
(FROM FRONT)

Purpose: Defensive players prevent penetration from the top of the key and then recover to their own guarded player if possible.

Number of Personnel: Minimum of four players to a maximum of twelve plus a coach.

Equipment and Facilities: A half court and a minimum of one basketball.

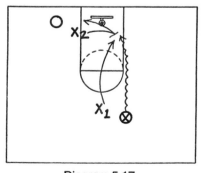

Diagram 5.17

Procedure: The defensive player by the top of the key allows dribbler to go by and then recovers with help from teammate (see Diagram 5.17). The defensive player by the baseline must stop dribbler and learn to take the charge. If player does not get charge, he or she must recover quickly to guard partner.

Time: A minimum of 5 minutes to a maximum of 15, if there is a large number of players.

Coaching Points: See Appendix B–II, Off-the-Ball Defense.

THREE-ON-THREE DRILL

Purpose: Offensive and defensive players work on proper three-on-three basketball techniques.

Number of Personnel: A minimum of six players to a maximum of twelve and a coach.

Equipment and Facilities: A half court and at least one basketball.

Procedure: Offensive players work on constant movement without the basketball. Coach can limit offensive players to no, one or two dribbles, and must make sure players are either cutting to the basket or screening for a teammate. Defensive players work on staying in their defensive stance, making cutters cut behind them, their position with relation to the ball, and talking loudly to teammates—calling out picks, cutter, help, etc.

Time: Whatever time limit is desired by the coach.

Coaching Points: See Appendix B–I, On-the-Ball Defense; Appendix B–II, Off-the-Ball Defense.

PHYSICAL CHECK AND RECOVER DRILL

Purpose: Defensive players learn proper techniques for defending a screen on the ball.

Number of Personnel: A minimum of four players to a maximum of eight and a coach.

Equipment and Facilities: A half court and one basketball.

Procedure: The defensive player guarding the player with the ball at the top of the key must fight over the screen and stay with the dribbler. Player must get help from teammate. The defensive player against screener must step out and check offensive dribbler and recover to his or her own player rolling to the basket (see Diagrams 5.18, 5.19). Coach can add a screen on other side of foul line so that dribbler may go off either player (see Diagram 5.19).

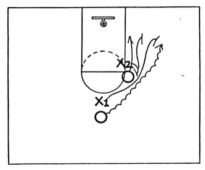

Diagram 5.18

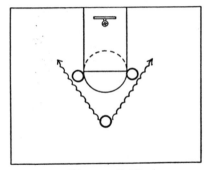

Diagram 5.19

Time: Minimum of 3 minutes to a maximum of 10.

Coaching Points: See Appendix B–II, Off-the-Ball Defense.

DEFENSIVE GAME DRILL

Purpose: Defense rewarded for preventing a score in a competitive situation.

Number of Personnel: Minimum of six players to a maximum of fifteen and a coach.

Equipment and Facilities: A half court and at least one basketball.

Procedure: All defensive players start under basket, and offensive players start at spot 1 (see Diagram 5.20). A defensive player who is stationed under the basket rolls the ball to an offensive player in the corner at spot 1. The offensive player should receive ball about two steps before defensive player gets there. Offensive player has only two dribbles. If offense scores, then defense stays in the defensive line under the basket, and offense goes to next spot. An offensive player who does not score goes to the defensive line, and a defensive player who prevents a score goes to whichever spot he or she left

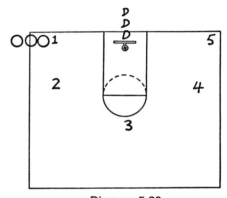

Diagram 5.20

off with as an offensive player. A player is finished with the drill after scoring from spot 5. The coach continues the drill until there is only one player left. Coach should have the last player run.

Time: Will depend upon the number of participating players.

Coaching Points: See Appendix B–I, On-the-Ball Defense; Appendix A–VI, Outside Moves.

JUMP AND FRONT DRILL

Purpose: Defensive player works on hustling back on defense to get ahead of the player with the ball and try to prevent a basket. Excellent conditioning drill.

Number of Personnel: A minimum of six players to a maximum of twenty, in pairs, and a coach.

Equipment and Facilities: A full court and preferably a ball for each set of partners. Coach may wish to have a whistle to begin each pair of players in the drill.

Procedure: At whistle, the offensive player dribbles as quickly as possible to half court and then goes directly to basket (see Diagram 5.21). The defensive

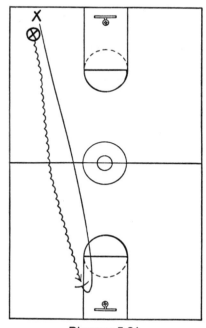

Diagram 5.21

player catches up to the offensive player and gets in front in order to turn him or her. The defensive player starts out about three steps behind the offensive player. Players will switch assignments when coming back down the court.

Time: A minimum of 3 minutes. Time length will depend on the number of players involved in the drill.

Coaching Points: See Appendix B–I, On-the-Ball Defense.

TRIANGLE DRILL

Purpose: Improvement of defensive footwork. Also good for conditioning.

Number of Personnel: Any number of players.

Equipment and Facilities: A half court.

Procedure: Players begin by shuffling to the corner (see Diagram 5.22). They do not cross their feet or let them touch. As they reach the corner, they push off from their outside foot and sprint toward the coach. They then sprint backwards with their heads high. Coach can repeat process as many times as desired.

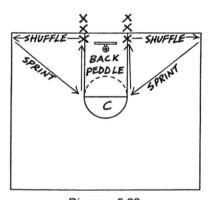

Diagram 5.22

Time: Will depend on the number of players. If there is a very small number, players may become quickly fatigued.

Coaching Points: Maintain defensive stance, knees flexed, and head and eyes up looking forward.

GUTS DRILL

Purpose: Players hustle after a loose ball and accustom themselves to diving on the floor. Defensive player is working on good on-the-ball defense and quick reaction.

Number of Personnel: Minimum of two players to a maximum of twenty and a coach.

Equipment and Facilities: A minimum of two baskets and balls.

Procedure: Coach rolls ball toward foul line to start the drill (see Diagram 5.23). Two players race after it until one gets possession. Coach then calls out a number of a basket and other player must prevent opponent from scoring.

Time: A minimum of 3 minutes.

Coaching Points: Players should go aggressively to the ball. Be sure that players are matched up according to size.

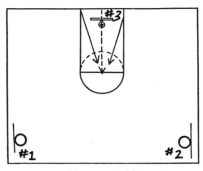
Diagram 5.23

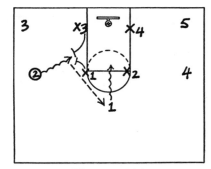
Diagram 5.24

FIVE-ON-FOUR DRILL

Purpose: Defensive players learn to cut off offensive penetration from the perimeter.

Number of Personnel: A minimum of nine players to a maximum of twenty and a coach.

Equipment and Facilities: A half court and one basketball.

Procedure: The five players on offense must attempt to score by driving for the hoop (see Diagram 5.24). The defense's objective is to jam the lane and force the ball handler to pick up dribble and pass ball out. The receiver of the pass in turn attempts to dribble through the defense and score. The drill continues for a set period or until the offense scores.

Time: A minimum of 5 minutes to a maximum of 15, depending on the number of participating players.

Coaching Points: See Appendix B–IV, Zone Defense Fundamentals.

KICK-OUT DRILL

Purpose: Defensive players work on jumping the player with a ball on a double team and learning to rotate the defensive help.

Number of Personnel: A minimum of six players to a maximum of twelve and a coach.

Equipment and Facilities: A half court and one basketball.

Procedure: Player A begins the drill by dribbling away from teammates (see Diagram 5.25). As A dribbles, X2 leaves the player he or she is guarding and comes from behind to trap. X1 forces A to turn into X2; X2 must either tie up dribbler or steal the ball. X1 and X2 avoid giving A enough room to get between them. X3 must anticipate A's attempted pass to B.

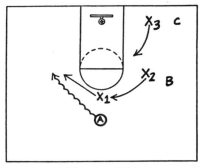

Diagram 5.25

Time: A minimum of 3 minutes to a maximum of 10.

Coaching Points: Coach must emphasize the proper rotations of the defensive personnel. See Appendix B–I, On-the-Ball Defense.

TOWEL DRILL

Purpose: Improve foot movement in playing on-the-ball defense by forbidding defensive players to use their hands.

Number of Personnel: Minimum of two players to a maximum of twenty and a coach.

Equipment and Facilities: A full court and a basketball, plus a towel for each pair of players.

Procedure: The defensive player assumes a good stance about four feet from the offensive player. Defender grasps one end of a towel with left hand

and the other end with right hand behind back. The offensive player dribbles down the floor. The defensive player must stay between the offensive player and the basket. Defender should try to maintain a constant distance from the offensive player. Players switch assignments when they come back up the court. The coach may want to limit the offensive player to using only half of the court.

Time: A minimum of 5 minutes to a maximum of 10.

Coaching Points: See Appendix B–I, On-the-Ball Defense.

GO DRILL

Purpose: Defensive player works on speed to beat offensive player to a spot and learns to take a charge. Offensive player learns to move to the basket for possible three-point play.

Number of Personnel: A minimum of two players to a maximum of twenty plus a coach.

Equipment and Facilities: A half court, at least two basketballs, and tape to mark spot on floor.

Procedure: The coach beings drill by yelling "Go" and throwing the ball to a player running to the basket from the right line (see Diagram 5.26). Defensive player also starts running on "Go." Defense must beat offense to the spot marked on the floor. The defensive player establishes position and draws the charge. Offensive player takes the ball hard to the basket to try for a three-point play.

Time: At least 3 minutes to a maximum of 10.

Coaching Points: In order to insure proper safety for players, the coach may elect to decrease the distance the offensive and defensive people must run. See Appendix B–II, Off-the-Ball Defense; Appendix A–II, Shooting.

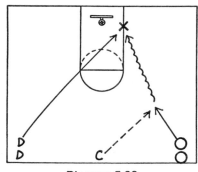

Diagram 5.26

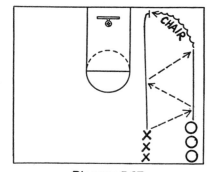

Diagram 5.27

CHARGE DRILL

Purpose: Players work on handling the basketball on passes and then reacting to make proper offensive and defensive plays.

Number of Personnel: Minimum of two players to a maximum of twenty and a coach.

Equipment and Facilities: A half court, one basketball, and a chair.

Procedure: A chair is placed about two to three feet outside the free-throw lane and about six feet from baseline (see Diagram 5.27). Offensive player begins about three steps in front of the defensive player. To begin drill, Player X passes to O and the ball is returned for second pass. O receives third pass just prior to making cut around chair, and drives to the basket for a lay-up. X speeds to the baseline for good defensive positioning to draw the charge.

Time: A minimum of 3 minutes to a maximum of 10.

Coaching Points: See Appendix B–II, Off-the-Ball Defense.

TOSS-IT-OUT-AND-PLAY
DIRECTIONAL DEFENSE DRILL

Purpose: For defense to learn to control the court.

Number of Personnel: A minimum of two players to a maximum of twenty and a coach. Players should be paired.

Equipment and Facilities: A half court and at least two basketballs. Best to have one ball per pair of players.

Procedure: Player X starts with the ball underneath the basket and passes it to O, who is waiting by the foul line (see Diagram 5.28). Player O must make offense do one of the following four moves as dictated by the coach:

(A) go left

(B) go right

(C) use weak hand

(D) shoot outside

The coach could run two offensive lines and two defensive lines on the same half court or could do it with one line each.

Time: At least 5 minutes to a maximum of 10 minutes.

Coaching Points: See Appendix B–I, On-the-Ball Defense.

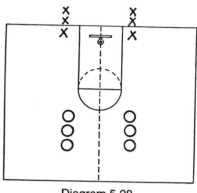

Diagram 5.28

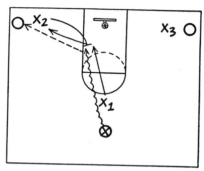

Diagram 5.29

STOP PENETRATION
AND RECOVER DRILL

Purpose: Teach defensive players to stop offensive penetration from the top of the key and to recover to contest a jump shooter.

Number of Personnel: Minimum of six players to a maximum of twelve and a coach.

Equipment and Facilities: A half court and one basketball.

Procedure: Drill uses three offensive and three defensive players. The offensive player at top of the key starts with ball (see Diagram 5.29), and makes a good one-on-one penetration on defensive player. The other two defensive players jump off their players and check the player with the ball. On a pass off to a corner player by the penetrator, the defensive player who checked recovers quickly to guard against a jump shot.

Time: A minimum of 3 minutes to a maximum of 10.

Coaching Points: See Appendix B–II, Off-the-Ball Defense.

CONVERSION DRILL OFF FOUL SHOT

Purpose: Teach players to return to a desired defense as quickly as possible.

Number of Personnel: A minimum of ten to a maximum of twenty players and a coach.

Equipment and Facilities: A full court and one basketball.

Procedure: Players practice getting back on defense. The team the coach wishes to work with shoots a foul shot. The other team will break immediately off a make or a miss. The defense is called by the coach each time a foul is shot. The coach could also work on conversion by letting players play five-on-five and on a whistle the offensive team drops the ball and hustles back on defense. The defensive team then tries to fast break for a score.

Time: From 5 to 10 minutes.

Coaching Points: Be sure that everyone hustles back to stop the break. All five players should try to get even with the ball and one player must pick up the ball.

CONVERSION DRILL OFF DUMMY

Purpose: Players work on getting back on defense quickly and effectively.

Number of Personnel: A minimum of ten players to a maximum of twenty and a coach.

Equipment and Facilities: A full court and one basketball.

Procedure: The coach chooses a team to run a specific offense on a dummy (no defense) basis. As soon as they shoot or the coach blows the whistle the other team, which is waiting along the baseline, picks up the ball and breaks as quickly as possible.

Time: 5 to 10 minutes.

Coaching Points: Be sure that everyone hustles back to stop the break. All five players should try to get even with the ball and one player must pick up the ball.

SHUFFLE CONTEST

Purpose: Players work on proper defensive footwork in a competitive situation.

Number of Personnel: A minimum of nine players to a maximum of twelve and a manager or coach.

Equipment and Facilities: A half court, one basketball, and a stopwatch.

Procedure: Four players (the Os) set up an equal distance (approximately eight feet) from a ball placed in the middle of the foul line (see Diagram 5.30). They are positioned to constantly face the point out front. One player holds the ball in the middle. Four players hold designated spots and count for the players running the drill. On a whistle, players shuffle and touch the ball and shuffle back to touch a counting player. They get one point for each time they touch the counter.

Time: Each time the drill is done for four players, it takes one minute. If twelve players complete the drill it will take a total of 3 minutes.

Coaching Points: See Appendix B–I, On-the-Ball Defense.

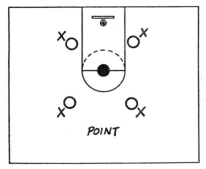

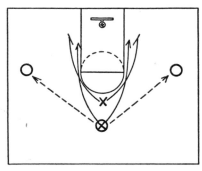

Diagram 5.30   Diagram 5.31

FRONT-THE-CUTTER DRILL

Purpose: Defensive player concentrates on getting off and toward the ball as soon as offensive player he or she is guarding makes a pass, in order to prevent the give-and-go move.

Number of Personnel: At least four players to a maximum of eight and a coach.

Equipment and Facilities: A half court and one basketball.

Procedure: The offensive player at the top of the key passes to either of the two wings (see Diagram 5.31). Player then cuts immediately to the basket looking for a give-and-go. The defensive player must prevent the offensive player from getting the ball on the give-and-go move. As soon as ball leaves offensive player's hands, the defensive player jumps off the player being guarded in the direction of the pass. Player must try to make the offensive player cut behind. Offensive player continues out to ball-side box on foul lane. When offense tries to post up and receive a pass, defensive player must continue to front. The coach should rotate the assignments of all four players.

Time: At least 3 minutes to a maximum of 10.

Coaching Points: See Appendix B–II, Off-the-Ball Defense.

TURN-THE-CORNER DRILL

Purpose: Defensive players work on quick foot movement and preventing an offensive player from beating them in an open court.

Number of Personnel: Minimum of two to a maximum of sixteen and a coach. Players should be in pairs.

Equipment and Facilities: A half court and preferably one basketball per pair.

Procedure: The coach establishes an area of the court where there are two boundary lines on each side and a finish line (see Diagram 5.32). Two players start directly between the two side boundary lines. The offensive player tries to dribble to the finish line, and, at the beginning of the drill, may go in only one direction. If the player starts driving to the right, then he or she must continue in that direction. Defensive player tries to beat offensive player to either of the side boundaries before he or she reaches the finish line. At a later time, the coach could allow the offensive player to change direction either once or twice.

Time: A minimum of 3 minutes to a maximum of 10 minutes if there are sixteen players doing the drill.

Coaching Points: See Appendix B–I, On-the-Ball Defense.

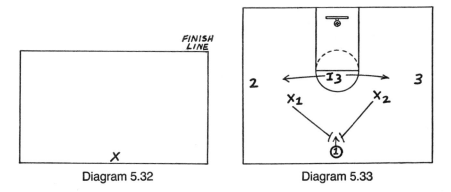

Diagram 5.32   Diagram 5.33

INTERCEPT-THE-PASS DRILL

Purpose: Work on defensive double-team pressure and anticipation of the interceptor. Offensive players work on passing skills.

Number of Personnel: A minimum of six players to a maximum of twelve and a coach.

Equipment and Facilities: A half court and one basketball.

Procedure: The drill uses three offensive and three defensive players. Player 1 in Diagram 5.33 dribbles across the half court line. Two defensive players (X1, and X2) attack 1 to double-team. Player 1 tries passing to either 2 or 3. The defensive players double-teaming work on proper technique—following the ball with their hands, locking feet, not allowing offensive player to split them, and so on. Offensive players 2 and 3 may not move. I3 is the third defensive player who tries to intercept any pass from 1 to 2 or 3. The coach should rotate players so that each player has a chance at each spot.

Time: A minimum of 5 minutes, longer if there is a large number of participating players.

Coaching Points: See Appendix B–II, Off-the-Ball Defense.

TWO-BALL QUICK-REACTION DRILLS

Purpose: Defensive player works on denying a pass into the post area, reacting to give help, and on-the-ball defense. Offensive player moves to the basket for a score.

Number of Personnel: From three to nine players and a coach.

Equipment and Facilities: A half court and two basketballs.

Procedure: The coach gets in position shown in Diagram 5.34A with two basketballs. In Diagram 5.34A, the offensive player flashes toward the high post. The defensive player must defend and knock pass away from the coach. The coach passes to the offensive player in the low post and the defensive player reacts quickly to give help. The low-post player makes a power move to the basket. In Diagram 5.34B, the coach makes a pass to the low-post player first with the defensive player reacting to help quickly. The coach then throws a second pass to a wing player floating to high post. The defensive player must react quickly to guard wing, who will try to go one-on-one. Coach should rotate the players in the drill.

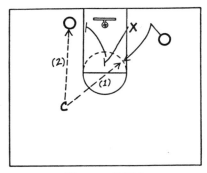

Diagram 5.34A

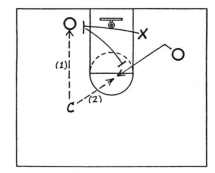

Diagram 5.34B

Time: A minimum of 5 minutes to a maximum of 10.

Coaching Points: Appendix B–II, Off-the-Ball Defense; Appendix A–IV, Inside Moves; Appendix A–VI, Outside Moves.

PICK-IT-UP DRILL

Purpose: Defensive players learn denial techniques against a spread offense while offensive players try to maintain control of the basketball. Defensive player guards and harasses the offensive player who picks up the dribble.

Number of Personnel: A minimum of ten players to a maximum of fifteen and a coach.

Equipment and Facilities: A half court and one basketball.

Procedure: Drill is comprised of a five-on-five situation with the five offensive players trying to hold the ball, in a four-corner setup. The defensive players try to force a jump ball. The defensive player guarding the person with the ball tries to force him or her to pick up the dribble, and then makes it difficult to pass. Whenever an offensive player picks up the dribble, the other four defensive players must deny the ball to the player they are guarding. Players should remember that the further their players are away from the ball, the further they may be away from the player they are covering. They should always be able to see both the ball and the offensive player they are covering. The coach should emphasize the ball-you-man principle. The coach may also facilitate the drill by yelling "pick it up" which keys offensive player to pick up the dribble.

Time: A minimum of 5 minutes to a maximum of 15.

Coaching Points: See Appendix B–II, Off-the-Ball Defense; Appendix B–I, On-the-Ball Defense.

DEFENDING THE WEAK-SIDE FLASH

Purpose: Drill teaches defense the following skills: denying a pass to the wing, jumping off guarded player towards the ball when pass is made to opposite side of the court, and fronting cutters across the lane area.

Number of Personnel: At least four players to a maximum of eight and a coach.

Equipment and Facilities: A half court and one basketball.

Procedure: The drill starts with three offensive players (two wings and a point player) and one defensive player on one of the wings (see Diagram 5.35). The defensive player denies pass to the wing. The point looks to make pass to that wing in order to make defensive player play "honestly." Point then makes a pass to the other wing. The weak-side wing cuts to either the low post or high post on ballside. The defensive player's job is to jump off guarded player toward the ball as soon as point passes to the other wing and front the cutter across the lane. Coach should rotate the positions of the players.

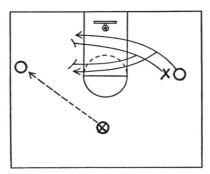

Diagram 5.35

Time: A minimum of 3 minutes to a maximum of 10.

Coaching Points: See Appendix B–II, Off-the-Ball Defense.

TWO-PLAYER
DEFENSIVE REACTION DRILLS

Purpose: Defensive wings work on proper positioning according to the movement of the basketball.

Number of Personnel: A minimum of four players to a maximum of eight and a coach.

Equipment and Facilities: A half court and one basketball.

Procedure: The coach has a basketball out front and dribbles from side to side in both drills. In Diagram 5.36A, defensive wings must react to where the ball is dribbled. The only move the offensive wings may make is a backdoor cut. In Diagram 5.36B, the offensive players work in the low post area, moving constantly and exchanging or screening for one another. Defensive players deny pass into the post by maintaining a fronting position. In

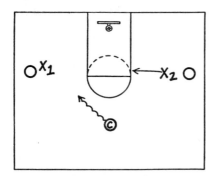

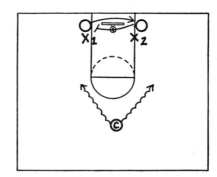

Diagram 5.36A   Diagram 5.36B

both drills, after a period of time, the coach switches players from offense to defense and vice versa.

Time: A minimum of 3 minutes to a maximum of 10.

Coaching Points: See Appendix B–II, Off-the-Ball Defense.

CREATIVE DEFENSIVE DRILL

Purpose: Players working on offensive and defensive skills involved in a three-on-three or four-on-four competitive situation.

Number of Personnel: A minimum of nine players to a maximum of fifteen and a coach and/or manager.

Equipment and Facilities: A half court, one basketball, and a stopwatch.

Procedure: The coach splits team into three- or four-player squads. The game is to three points. Offense gets one point for each basket they score, and defense gets a point for each turnover they force and for each defensive rebound they grab. Losers run a 30-second line drill while a new squad comes on the floor. Winning team continues to play but switches assignments—if they were defense, they become offense, and vice versa.

Time: As long as the coach desires.

Coaching Points: See Appendix A–VIII, Setting and Using Screens; Appendix B–II, Off-the-Ball Defense.

DEFENSIVE STANCE AND SHUFFLE DRILL

Purpose: Gives the players the fundamentals of a defensive stance, and proper foot movement while maintaining the stance. Drill is also good for conditioning players.

Number of Personnel: Any number of players and a coach.

Equipment and Facilities: At least a half court, possibly a full court if number of participating players in the drill demands.

Procedure: Players line up in sets of four, spread out over the court, facing the coach (see Diagram 5.37). The players are to assume and maintain a good defensive stance. The coach points in the direction he desires them to shuffle (left or right). Players should not cross their feet or allow them to touch. The coach may point for them to move backwards in a retreat step. In order to execute the retreat, a player should pivot on the back foot, swing the front leg behind it, and then shuffle backwards. If coach points forward, then players sprint towards him or her. Players must keep their heads up and react quickly to the coach's commands.

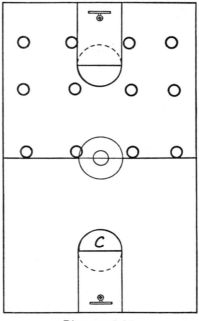

Diagram 5.37

Time: A minimum of 3 minutes to a maximum of 10. Coach may want to give breaks during the drill and then repeat it.

Coaching Points: See Appendix B–I, On-the-Ball Defense.

DEFENSIVE REACTION DRILL

Purpose: Players work on defensive fundamentals while reacting to a leader making various offensive moves.

Number of Personnel: Any number of players and a coach.

Equipment and Facilities: At least a half court and possibly a full court if necessitated by the number of players.

Procedure: One player stands in front of the others and runs the drill. The coach may have team captain lead the drill or may designate a new player each day. Other players spread out over the court and face Player 1 (see Diagram 5.38). They react to whatever the leader decides to do. The leader's options are to

1. dribble to the left—defense shuffles to the right
2. dribble to the right—defense shuffles to the left

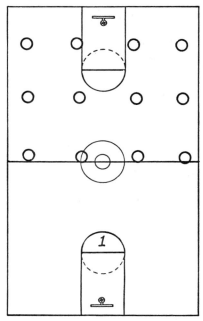

Diagram 5.38

3. dribble forward—defense retreats

4. dribble backwards—defense advances

5. shoot—defense jumps vertically with arms extended and yells "Shot." (When defensive players land they pivot with elbows out in proper box-out position. They then pivot back and wait for leader's next move.)

6. fake a shot—defensive players do *not* leave their feet

7. roll or drop basketball on floor—defensive players dive on the floor as if they were getting a loose ball. They then get back up quickly in order to be able to react to leader's next move.

Time: As long as coach desires.

Coaching Points: See Appendix B–I, On-the-Ball Defense.

RUN, SLIDE, RUN DRILL

Purpose: Defensive players learn to turn the offensive players they are guarding in an open court situation.

Number of Personnel: From two to twenty players, paired according to ability, if possible, and a coach.

Equipment and Facilities: A full-court and preferably a basketball per pair.

Procedure: The drill uses two players, offensive and defensive. The offensive player dribbles with the left hand when going left and right hand when going right. The defensive player alternates a run with a slide. When they reach the corner at the opposite end of the court, both players slide to spot indicated on Diagram 5.39. They then change assignments from offense to defense and vice versa and proceed down the court using the same techniques. In Diagram 5.39, the defensive player runs to the right and slides to the left. On their alternate trips up and down the court, the coach may have players slide first and then run.

Time: Whatever time coach desires.

Coaching Points: See Appendix B–I, On-the-Ball Defense.

BLOCK-THE-SHOT DRILL

Procedure: Players learn to contest a shooter without fouling, and not to leave the floor until the shooter does so.

Number of Personnel: At least two players to a maximum of six players per half court. Players should be in pairs.

Equipment and Facilities: A half court and a basketball per pair if possible. The more baskets the coach has to work with, the more effective the drill will be.

Procedure: The coach matches up players according to size and puts them in pairs. To start the drill, the offensive players get no dribbles, but are able to establish a pivot foot. The objective of the defense is to block the offensive player's shot. Each player shoots ten times, and should be charted on number of shots made each time the drill is run. The defensive player must not leave the floor until the offensive player leaves the ground to shoot, but should extend one arm straight up in the attempt to block. After players have done drill with no dribble, they then may take one dribble, then two dribbles. The coach should emphasize proper defensive block-out technique and rushing to the board for the rebound. After offense takes ten shots, players switch assignments.

Time: However long it takes each player to shoot at least thirty shots.

Coaching Points: See Appendix B–I, On-the-Ball Defense; Appendix A–II, Shooting; Appendix B–III, Defensive Rebounding.

HANDS DRILL

Purpose: Defensive players learn proper hand technique in harassing an offensive player with the ball.

Number of Personnel: From two to twenty players, in pairs.

Equipment and Facilities: A ball for each pair of players.

Procedure: Two players face each other approximately an arm's length apart. Offensive player has a basketball and moves it, keeping ball in front and no higher than the chest. Defensive player assumes defensive stance and moves hands up to knock ball away from offensive player. After one minute players reverse roles.

Time: 2 minutes.

Coaching Points: See Appendix B–I, On-the-Ball Defense.

ONE-ON-ONE, FULL-COURT DRILL

Purpose: Defense practices high-pressure, player-to-player, full-court defense, trying to beat the offensive player to a spot and turn him or her with the basketball. Offense works on ball handling skills while protecting the basketball. A very good conditioning drill.

Number of Personnel: From two to twenty-four players and a coach.

Equipment and Facilities: A full court and a basketball for every two players.

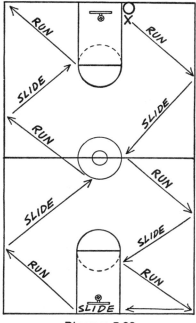

Diagram 5.39

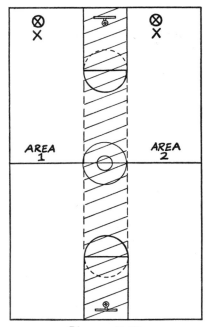

Diagram 5.40

Procedure: Players of approximately equal size, ability, and speed are paired up for this drill. The full court is divided into three areas for the drill: Area 1 and Area 2 (see Diagram 5.40) are the sections to be utilized for the drill. The shaded area in Diagram 5.40 is not to be used by the players. The offensive player begins at one baseline and tries to cross the other baseline, remaining in his or her area of the court, without losing the basketball. The defensive player works to prevent the offensive player from achieving that goal, concentrating on quick foot movement in order to maintain proper body position against the offensive player. Defense must not reach and uses his or her hands to steal the basketball only when the offensive player gives the opportunity by not protecting the ball. When players reach the opposite baseline they stay there and then switch roles when coming back down the court.

Time: 3 to 10 minutes.

Coaching Points: See Appendix B–I, On-the-Ball Defense; Appendix A–I, Ball Handling.

ZONE REACTION DRILL

Purpose: Defense practices reacting to offense's quick movement of the basketball. They also learn to pressure the player with the basketball and to cut off scoring opportunities. Offensive players practice passing skills and quick ball movement.

Number of Personnel: Five players and a coach.

Equipment and Facilities: A half court and one basketball.

Procedure: The drill utilizes three offensive players; one on each box along a foul lane and the third at the foul line. They are to remain stationary. Two defensive players set up in a tandem in the foul lane (see Diagram 5.41A). The drill starts with the ball in the hands of the offensive player at the foul line, who may pass to either player stationed on a foul-lane box. On the pass, the back defensive player in the tandem goes to pressure the person receiving the pass. The defensive player guarding the person at the foul line must drop quickly to cut off the quick pass to the offensive player on the opposite box. When the offensive person on the box with the basketball passes back out to a teammate at the foul line, the defensive players react quickly to form the tandem once again. The defensive player opposite the ball should be the one to go guard the person with the basketball at the foul line (see Diagram 5.41B). Defensive players should communicate with one another on their coverages and continue to work hard for the duration of the drill. The offensive players on the boxes may shoot the basketball only if they are left wide open by defensive players who are very slow to react. The coach must make sure that all players get a chance to play defense.

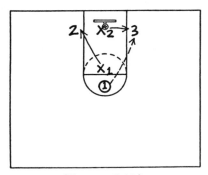

Diagram 5.41A

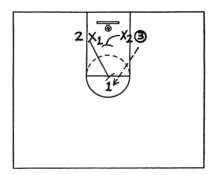

Diagram 5.41B

Time: Each pair of defensive players should drill for 30 seconds to 1 minute. Total time to be allotted for the completion of the drill should not exceed 6 minutes.

Coaching Points: See Appendix B–IV, Zone Defense Fundamentals.

DEFENSIVE SHUFFLE DRILL

Purpose: To teach players the proper defensive stance and foot movement associated with a defensive shuffle. Emphasis is on players staying low and not letting their feet touch or cross.

Number of Personnel: The drill is designed for one player at a time. A person to keep time and record the score of the player is also needed.

Equipment and Facilities: A space approximately twelve feet square, two shallow boxes, four whiffle balls, and a stopwatch.

Procedure: Two shallow boxes are placed about ten feet apart, each containing two whiffle balls. The player begins by standing next to one box and picking up one whiffle ball, shuffling immediately to the other box and dropping the ball into it. Player picks up another ball and shuffles back to the first box. The process continues for a set period of time. The player earns one point for each time a whiffle ball is dropped in a box. In order to get the point, player must use a defensive shuffle and cannot run from box to box. The drill can be used as a competition among several players or as a way for a single player to improve quickness while doing a defensive shuffle.

Time: 30 to 60 seconds.

Coaching Points: See Appendix B–I, On-the-Ball Defense.

SHOOTING DRILLS

TEAM SPOT-SHOOTING DRILL

Purpose: Players practice shooting from various spots on the floor in a competitive situation.

Number of Personnel: From four to sixteen players per half court.

Equipment and Facilities: At least one half court; more baskets will make the drill run more smoothly. Also need one basketball per team.

Procedure: All players start at Spot 1. The coach divides players into three or four teams. If a player makes a shot from Spot 1, he or she gets own rebound and dribbles to the next spot (see Diagram 6.1). Player must always get his or her own rebound and, if unsuccessful, must pass to the next member of the team. A player who misses from Spot 9 must start over again beginning at Spot 1. The coach or manager adds up the points (spot each player on a team has completed) for each team to decide the winner if drill is run on a time limit, and can also decide to make the winner the first team to have two, three, or four players finished.

Time: Coach could run the drill for a set time period—from 5 to 10 minutes. Otherwise, time will depend upon how quickly players complete the cycle.

Coaching Points: See Appendix A–II, Shooting.

RAPID-FIRE DRILL

Purpose: Work on the following fundamentals: rebounding and outletting the basketball, passing to a target, getting behind the ball before a shot, getting in good balance position when shooting the basketball.

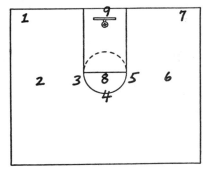

Diagram 6.1

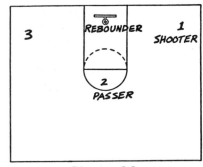

Diagram 6.2

Number of Personnel: Three players per basket and a coach or manager.

Equipment and Facilities: As many baskets as possible with three players to a basket, two basketballs per three-player group, and a stopwatch for the coach or manager.

Procedure: The drill begins with a shooter, a passer, and a rebounder as shown in Diagram 6.2. The shooter has one basketball and the passer the other. The shooter must keep moving at all times. He or she first shoots without dribbling and later the coach may add shooting off of the crossover dribble or reverse dribble, and so on. After the shooter has shot for one minute, the players rotate positions: the shooter becomes the rebounder, the rebounder becomes the passer, and the passer becomes the shooter. After everyone has shot once from Spot 1, then Spot 2 will be shot from, and then Spot 3. The passer should work on both bounce and chest passes.

Time: Each of the three players at a basket shoots for 1 minute from each of three spots indicated on diagram. It should take a total of 9 minutes to run through entire drill.

Coaching Points: See Appendix A–II, Shooting; Appendix A–V, Passing and Receiving Passes.

WOODY DRILL

Purpose: The following fundamentals are stressed during the drill: rebounding and outletting the basketball, contesting a shooter, and shooting on balance while someone is guarding the shooter.

Number of Personnel: Three players per basket.

Equipment and Facilities: A basket for each group of three players and one basketball.

Procedure: Player 1 shoots the basketball, guarded by X3 (see Diagram

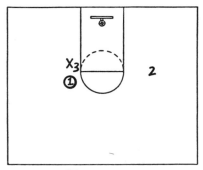

Diagram 6.3

6.3). X3 rebounds the shot and makes a strong outlet pass to 2. As soon as 1 takes the shot, he or she moves quickly to play defense on 2. Player 1 then rebounds 2's shot and makes an outlet pass to X3. After 2 takes the shot, he or she plays defense on X3. The players continue the process for the duration of the drill.

Time: Coach may run drill for any time desired.

Coaching Points: Coach must watch the spacing of the players. The shorter the distance the easier the drill will be. See Appendix A–II, Shooting; Appendix B–I, On-the-Ball Defense; Appendix B–II, Defensive Rebounding.

TWO-PLAYER SHOOTING DRILL

Purpose: Shooter works on shooting the basketball off of various offensive moves, and concentrates on stamina.

Number of Personnel: Two players per basket.

Equipment and Facilities: A basket and a basketball for every two players.

Procedure: The shooter will go for a total of twenty-five shots (see Diagram 6.4). The rebounder must get the ball back to the shooter as quickly as possible. For the first ten shots, the shooter does not dribble, on the next five, he or she takes *one*. For the following five shots, shooter takes *two* dribbles and during the last set of five, he or she shoots off a spin dribble or off a crossover dribble. The shooter must keep moving around the perimeter during all twenty-five shots. The coach could have players do all twenty-five shots with no dribble first, then one dribble, and so on. The coach may also decide to operate the drill on a time limit as opposed to the twenty-five shots.

Time: Coach may run drill as many times and for whatever time desired.

Coaching Points: Coach should stress to rebounder the importance of making accurate passes to the shooter. See Appendix A–II, Shooting; Appendix A–V, Passing and Receiving Passes.

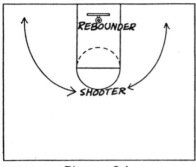

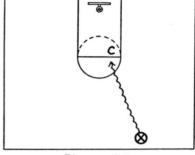

Diagram 6.4   Diagram 6.5

HUBIE BROWN SHOOTING DRILL #1

Purpose: Players learn the proper technique of pulling up off the dribble to shoot the jumper.

Number of Personnel: One to ten players and a coach per half court.

Equipment and Facilities: At least one half court and, preferably, a basketball for each player.

Procedure: Players take two or three dribbles from half court toward the coach at the corner of the foul line and pull up to take a jump shot (see Diagram 6.5). They keep their eyes on the rim and make the last bounce hard. The players get their own rebound and then go to opposite side at half court. Players make sure to go straight up, on balance, for the jumper and not drift into the coach.

Time: Coach may run drill for any time desired.

Coaching Points: See Appendix A–II, Shooting.

HUBIE BROWN SHOOTING DRILL #2

Purpose: Players practice squaring up to the basket and shooting the jumper on balance, off the dribble.

Number of Personnel: One to ten players and a coach per half court.

Equipment and Facilities: At least one half court, and preferably, a basketball for each player.

Procedure: Players step towards the baseline and then cross over and dribble towards the foul line (see Diagram 6.6). They make their last dribble hard and pull it around so that they are square to basket. They get their own rebound and go to the opposite foul line extended.

Time: Coach may run drill as long as desired.

Coaching Points: See Appendix A–II, Shooting.

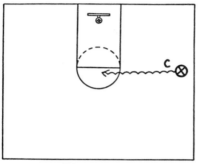   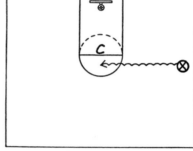

Diagram 6.6   Diagram 6.7

HUBIE BROWN SHOOTING DRILL #3

Purpose: Each offensive player learns how to shake a defensive guard by making a proper pivot and ball fake before taking the jumper.

Number of Personnel: One to ten players and a coach per half court.

Equipment and Facilities: At least one half court and a basketball for each player.

Procedure: Players step towards the baseline and cross over and dribble towards the foul line (see Diagram 6.7). They assume that the defensive player stays with them, so they plant their outside foot and use it as a pivot foot. They then give a ball fake and pivot around for jump shot. Players get their own rebound and go to the opposite foul line extended.

Time: Coach may run drill for as long as desired.

Coaching Points: See Appendix A–II, Shooting.

HUBIE BROWN SHOOTING DRILL #4

Purpose: Working on the baseline jump shot.

Number of Personnel: One to ten players and a coach per half court.

Equipment and Facilities: At least one half court, and a basketball for each player.

Procedure: Players dribble toward the baseline, making their last dribble hard and pulling the ball across their body so they are square to the basket (see Diagram 6.8). They get their own rebound and move to the opposite foul line extended.

Time: However long the coach desires.

Coaching Points: See Appendix A–II, Shooting.

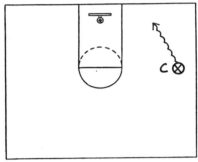
Diagram 6.8

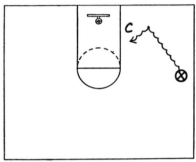
Diagram 6.9

HUBIE BROWN SHOOTING DRILL #5

Purpose: Players learn to reverse dribble on the baseline and use the backboard on their jump shot.

Number of Personnel: One to ten players and a coach per half court.

Equipment and Facilities: At least one half court, and a basketball for each player.

Procedure: Players assume that their defensive guard will beat them to the baseline to prevent the jumper. They pull the ball around for one reverse dribble, take one long step, and shoot a bank shot. They get their own rebound and go to the other side of the floor (see Diagram 6.9).

Time: However long the coach desires.

Coaching Points: See Appendix A–II, Shooting.

HUBIE BROWN SHOOTING DRILL #6

Purpose: Players learn to use a reverse dribble to go to the basket when overplayed by the defensive guard.

Number of Personnel: One to ten players and a coach per half court.

Equipment and Facilities: At least one half court, and a basketball for each player.

Procedure: Players take a step toward the baseline and then cross over and dribble toward the foul line (see Diagram 6.10). They assume the defensive guard will beat them to foul line. Players then execute a reverse dribble and keep the ball in the same hand. They take two steps and then do a power lay-up or baby hook. Players get their own rebound and go to the opposite foul line extended.

Time: However long the coach desires.

Coaching Points: See Appendix A–II, Shooting.

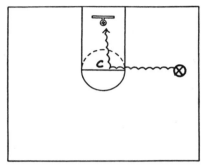
Diagram 6.10

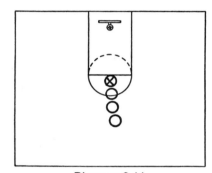
Diagram 6.11

JUMP-SHOT DRILL FROM FOUL LINE

Purpose: To practice jump shot from foul line area in a competitive situation.

Number of Personnel: Teams of no more than five at each basket.

Equipment and Facilities: As many baskets as possible and one basketball per team.

Procedure: The coach should divide the players up as evenly as possible at each basket being used. Player at the front of each line shoots jumper from foul line, rebounds his own shot, and passes to next player in line (see Diagram 6.11). Drill continues until one team has made twenty-one baskets, or the coach could decide to make it a best of three competition. Coach should have losers run.

Time: Time depends on how long it takes a team to make twenty-one baskets or complete the best of three competition.

Coaching Points: See Appendix A–II, Shooting.

TWENTY-ONE-JUMP-SHOT DRILL
FROM FOUL LINE AND CORNERS

Purpose: To practice jump shot from foul line and corners in a competitive situation.

Number of Personnel: Teams of three to six players per basket.

Equipment and Facilities: As many baskets as possible and three basketballs per basket.

Procedure: Coach should divide players up as evenly as possible among baskets. Each player marked on Diagram 6.12 has a ball. Each shooter rebounds his or her own shot and then goes back to the same spot. Drill continues until one team has made a total of twenty-one baskets, or the coach can make it a best of three competition. An alternative is to have each player shoot from all three spots and then take the total baskets made in three one-minute time periods to determine the team's score.

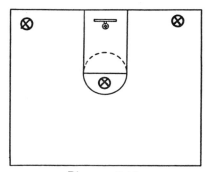

Diagram 6.12

Time: Time will depend on how coach chooses to run drill.

Coaching Points: See Appendix A–II, Shooting.

SHOOTING OFF TRIANGLE DRILL

Purpose: Players learn to execute a simple offense and work on the shots which present themselves while they run offense.

Number of Personnel: Three players per basket.

Equipment and Facilities: As many baskets as possible and a basketball per three-player group.

Procedure: Players run the "triangle" offense (see Diagrams 6.13A and B). The player with the basketball makes a pass across the foul line, goes down

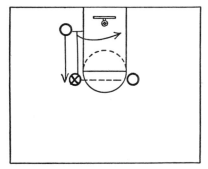

Diagram 6.13A

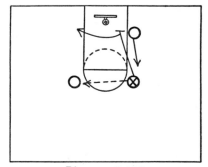

Diagram 6.13B

to set screen, and moves to the opposite box in the foul lane. Players continue to execute these movements in order to run the "triangle" offense. The players look to take the various shots which present themselves during the offense. They should work especially on the drive to the basket when a side is cleared for them, and on the jumper when they receive the pass at one side of the foul line.

Time: 3 to 10 minutes.

Coaching Points: See Appendix A–II, Shooting; Appendix A–VIII, Setting and Using Screens.

BASELINE JUMPER DRILL

Purpose: Players work on making accurate passes, shooting baseline jumpers, going to rebound the basketball, and making strong outlet passes.

Number of Personnel: Three players per basket.

Equipment and Facilities: As many baskets as possible and one basketball per three-player group.

Procedure: Player P is the passer, R is the rebounder, and S is the shooter (see Diagram 6.14). Drill begins with the passer throwing the ball to rebounder at the high post. On the pass to the high post, the shooter drifts toward the baseline. The rebounder turns to hit shooter with a good pass, rebounding each shot taken by the player on the baseline, and putting all misses in. Rebounder then fires an outlet pass to the passer and moves quickly back to the high post position. The process is then repeated, with players rotating assignments.

Time: Drill continues for as long as coach desires.

Coaching Points: See Appendix A–II, Shooting; Appendix A–V, Passing and Receiving Passes; Appendix B–III, Defensive Rebounding.

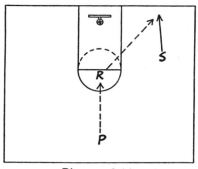

Diagram 6.14

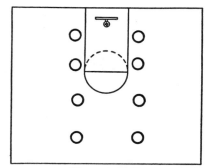

Diagram 6.15

FORM SHOOTING DRILL

Purpose: Players learn proper shooting techniques.

Number of Personnel: Any number of players and a coach.

Equipment and Facilities: A basketball for every two players.

Procedure: Players face each other and shoot a basketball back and forth among themselves, concentrating strictly on form (see Diagram 6.15). Coach moves among the players to correct any problems of technique.

Time: However long coach desires.

Coaching Points: See Appendix A–II, Shooting.

IMAGINARY-JUMP-SHOT DRILL

Purpose: To increase player shooting confidence.

Number of Personnel: Any number of players.

Equipment and Facilities: No special facilities or equipment are needed.

Procedure: Players can face either the coach or a basket. No balls are used in the drill. The players go through shooting motions and imagine that each shot taken goes in. They must imagine themselves being successful each time they shoot, and should mentally see the ball go in the basket.

Time: Time to be determined by coach.

Coaching Points: See Appendix A–II, Shooting.

SHOOTING OFF SPLIT DRILL

Purpose: Players practice proper techniques of running a split on a pass to a low post and shooting the basketball when they receive pass back from the post player.

Number of Personnel: Six to fourteen players per basket.

Equipment and Facilities: At least one basket and two basketballs.

Procedure: Drill is set up with posts on each side of the lane and two players with each post player (see Diagram 6.16). A distance of ten to twelve feet should be established between perimeter players and between the perimeter players and the post players. One perimeter player passes the ball into the post, then executes a split with the other perimeter player. They work on taking jump shots off the split. A point for players to remember: the passer into the post screens for the other perimeter player.

Time: To be determined by coach.

Coaching Points: See Appendix A–II, Shooting.

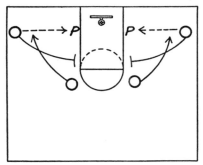
Diagram 6.16

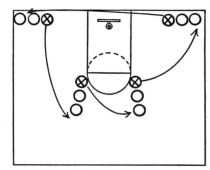
Diagram 6.17

PRE-GAME SHOOTING DRILL

Purpose: For the entire team to take a large number of shots while shooting from designated spots on the floor.

Number of Personnel: A minimum of eight players to a maximum of sixteen.

Equipment and Facilities: One basket and four basketballs.

Procedure: Players set up in the four lines shown in Diagram 6.17; the first player in each line has a basketball. After they shoot, they get their own rebound and pass ball to the next player in their line. The shooter then goes to the end of the next line in a counterclockwise direction. Coach may want to add a fifth spot at the foul line to work on foul shooting.

Time: A set period of time designated by the coach.

Coaching Points: See Appendix A–II, Shooting.

COMPETITIVE SHOOTING DRILL

Purpose: Players are working on their jump shot from the foul line area while in a competitive situation.

Number of Personnel: Four to sixteen players may participate.

Equipment and Facilities: One basket and two basketballs.

Procedure: Players set up in two lines at either side of the top of the key (see Diagram 6.18). They take one hard dribble toward the basket and pull up for an on-balance jump shot. They rebound their own shot and go to the end of the opposite line. The coach could run the same drill from each corner. The first line to reach twenty-one baskets wins. Losers must run a thirty-second line drill.

Time: Drill will last as long as it takes one line to make twenty-one baskets.

Coaching Points: See Appendix A–II, Shooting.

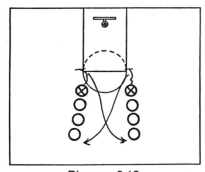

Diagram 6.18

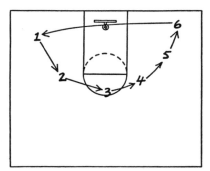

Diagram 6.19

CIRCLE SHOOTING DRILL

Purpose: To teach players to shoot from six designated spots on the floor while operating under a time limit, to be quick but unhurried.

Number of Personnel: One player shooting and possibly one player rebounding per basket.

Equipment and Facilities: A basket and a basketball for each shooting player.

Procedure: There are six spots on the floor shown in Diagram 6.19. Player starts at Spot 1 and moves as indicated in diagram. He or she must make a shot from each spot before moving to the next. Coach may have players do this drill with or without a rebounder. If there is no rebounder, shooter rebounds own shot and then dribbles to the spot where he or she is working.

Shooter should be able to hit a shot from nine spots well within a one-minute time period. If a rebounder is being used to pass ball back, then shooter should be able to reach at least eighteen spots in a one-minute time period.

Time: A 1-minute time period for each shooting player.

Coaching Points: See Appendix A–II, Shooting.

THREE TYPES OF SHOTS DRILL

Purpose: To teach players to shoot the baseline jumper, the bank shot, and jump shots from around the top of the key.

Number of Personnel: From three to five players per basket.

Equipment and Facilities: One basket for each group of players and two basketballs per group.

Procedure: Coach divides team into groups at separate baskets to work on three different types of shots. First is the baseline jumper (see Diagram 6.20A). Two players in line have a basketball. The first player in line shoots, rebounds his or her own shot, passes ball to next player in line without a ball, and then goes to opposite side. The first group to make fifteen baskets wins. The coach should get scores of the other groups. The second shot to be worked on is the bank shot (see Diagram 6.20B). Again, first two players in line have a basketball and follow same procedure as with first drill, although now they must bank the shot. Once again, the first group to get fifteen baskets wins. The coach again gets scores of the other groups. The third shot is from out front. Same procedure as previous drills except that after they shoot and rebound, players go to the next of the four spots indicated in Diagram 6.20C. The first team to make fifteen baskets wins. The coach again gets scores from the other groups and adds up the total scores for each group to determine the drill winner. Losers run a thirty-second drill.

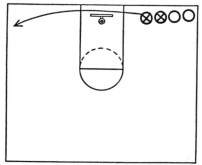

Diagram 6.20A

Diagram 6.20B

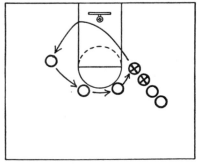

Diagram 6.20C

Time: Time depends on how long it takes the players to make all forty-five total shots.

Coaching Points: See Appendix A–II, Shooting.

LAY-UP JUMP-SHOT DRILL

Purpose: For conditioning and for teaching players to shoot both lay-ups and jump shots while fatigued.

Number of Personnel: Three players and a coach or manager per basket.

Equipment and Facilities: One basket and two basketballs per three-player group.

Procedure: Drill begins with the placement of a basketball on each corner of the foul line. Player 3 (see Diagram 6.21) should be facing the basket in about the middle of the lane. At the whistle of the coach or manager, 3 goes and gets the basketball to his or her right and drives in for a lay-up. Player 3 then gets the other basketball and shoots a jump shot, continuing the process

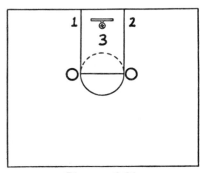

Diagram 6.21

for a set period of time. When 3 does drill a second time, he or she will shoot lay-up with the ball to the left and a jump shot with the ball to the right. 1 and 2 rebound each shot and place balls back to their original spots.

Time: Each player running through the drill will do it for a 30- to 60-second time period, determined by coach. Maximum time to complete drill would be six minutes per three-player group.

Coaching Points: See Appendix A–II, Shooting.

SPOT SHOOTING DRILL

Purpose: Players work on jump shots from five areas of the floor.

Number of Personnel: One player per basket.

Equipment and Facilities: A basket for each player and one basketball.

Procedure: Player shoots from each of the five areas labelled in Diagram 6.22 starting with Area 1. Player should run to get each rebound and then dribble back to a particular area, taking five shots from each area. Player's goal should be to make at least fifteen out of the twenty-five attempted shots. Player must work hard and go through drill at top speed.

Time: Time will depend on how long it takes a player to shoot twenty-five shots.

Coaching Points: See Appendix A–II, Shooting.

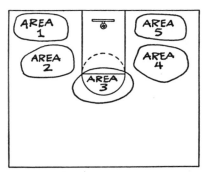

Diagram 6.22

FAKE-AND-SHOOT DRILL

Purpose: Players practice jump shots off of some type of offensive move from five areas of the floor.

Number of Personnel: One player per basket.

Equipment and Facilities: A basket for each player and one basketball.

Procedure: Player shoots five shots from each area labelled in Diagram 6.22, hustling after each shot to get the rebound and dribble back out to a particular spot. A player who gets to the area from which he or she is going to shoot squares up to the basket and makes a move before taking a shot. Example: jab step and one dribble to the right for the shot; jab step and cross-over; shoot off spin dribble; shoot off stop and go dribble; and so on. Player's goal should be to make at least fifteen out of twenty-five attempted shots. Drill must be done as if in game conditions.

Time: Time will depend on how long it takes a player to shoot a total of twenty-five shots.

Coaching Points: See Appendix A–II, Shooting.

EIGHT-AND-MOVE
COMPETITIVE DRILL

Purpose: For players to shoot from a wide range of spots on the basketball floor in a competitive situation.

Number of Personnel: From two to ten players per basket and a coach or manager.

Equipment and Facilities: A basket and a basketball for each group of players.

Procedure: Players in each group begin at Spot 1 and shoot until they make eight shots (see Diagram 6.23). Each group starts with a rebounder under the basket. The player who shoots becomes the next rebounder and each rebounder goes to the end of the line. After a group makes eight shots from one spot they move to the next spot. They should continue the process until the group has completed shooting at all seven spots. There will be a group of players

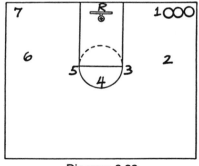

Diagram 6.23

at two or more baskets which would put the groups in competition with one another. Losers run.

Time: Time will depend upon how long it takes a group of players to make a total of fifty-six shots.

Coaching Points: See Appendix A–II, Shooting.

TWO-POST JUMP-SHOT DRILL

Purpose: Players learn to keep under control when going hard to the basket and pulling up for the jump shot. They concentrate on being on balance and going straight up for the jumper. This drill is also good for conditioning.

Number of Personnel: Ten to fourteen players and a coach or manager present at each basket in order to record the number of successful jump shots.

Equipment and Facilities: A full court for every ten to fourteen players. The coach must have a watch and a whistle. Two basketballs are needed for each full court used.

Procedure: To set up the drill, the coach places one player at each corner of the foul line of a full court (designated P in Diagram 6.24). The players that will be shooting the jump shots are divided evenly under each basket (S in the diagram). Jump shots will always be taken at the foul line. At the whistle by the coach, players begin drill. The first shooters in line at each basket start with jump shots at the foul line of their own baskets. They then rebound their own shots and pass the ball out to the post players nearest them and to their right. The shooters then sprint towards the other basket and receive a return pass from the post player. The shooters then make a long pass to the post player on the right at the other basket. The second post player now makes a return pass to the shooter before reaching the foul line. The shooter takes the jumper at the foul line. The next shooter comes from underneath the basket, gets the rebound and quickly passes the ball out to the post player to his or her right. The process is repeated and the drill continues.

During the course of the drill, the shooters periodically relieve the post players of their duties. This way all players get an opportunity to be shooters and post players. If the drill is done using two full courts at the same time the two groups will compete against one another. The group that succeeds in the least number of jump shots must run a 30-second line drill.

Time: From 2 to 5 minutes. Players should be able to make at least ten shots for the full court for each minute the drill is performed. Example: If the drill is done for 2 minutes, then there should be twenty shots made on the full court, 4 minutes then forty successful jump shots. If only one group is performing the drill, then the coach may wish to raise the goal for the

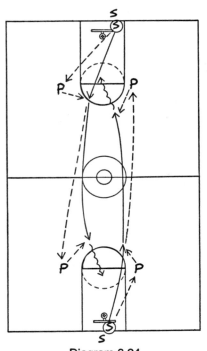

Diagram 6.24

given time period and instruct players that the drill does not end until the established goal has been accomplished.

Coaching Points: See Appendix A–II, Shooting; Appendix A–V, Passing and Receiving Passes.

CONTESTING-THE-JUMPER-
IN-THE-CORNER DRILL

Purpose: For players to get used to being run at by a defensive player when taking a jump shot from the baseline.

Number of Personnel: A minimum of six players to a maximum of eighteen.

Equipment and Facilities: At least two basketballs and a half court.

Procedure: The drill begins with Player 1 at the point passing the basketball to either wing. In Diagram 6.25 the pass went to Player 2. After 1 passes to 2, he or she follows the pass to the same side baseline. As soon as 2 receives the pass from 1, 2 passes to 3, who has already started to move toward the foul lane. Player 2 follows the pass so as to be positioned for a rebound, being careful not to interfere in 3's passing lane. When 3 catches the pass from 2, 3 immediately passes to 1 on the opposite baseline. Player 3 follows the pass and contests 1's jump shot but does *not* block it. Player 2 rebounds

1's shot and brings the basketball out to the line at the top of the key. The rotation of players is as follows: the rebounder (2) moves to the line at the point, the shooter (1) goes to the opposite wing, and the player contesting the shot (3) gets in the wing line nearest to where he or she ran at the shooter.

Time: 3 to 10 minutes.

Coaching Points: This drill can be effectively used in a pre-game warm-up situation. See Appendix A–II, Shooting.

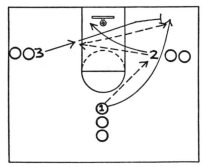

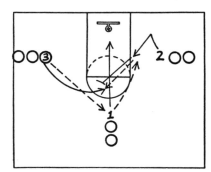

Diagram 6.25   Diagram 6.26

CONTESTING-THE-JUMPER-AT-THE-TOP DRILL

Purpose: For players to become accustomed to pressure from defensive players when taking a jump shot from the top of the key.

Number of Personnel: A minimum of six players to a maximum of eighteen.

Equipment and Facilities: At least two basketballs and a half court.

Procedure: The drill starts with the ball at either wing position. In Diagram 6.26 Player 3 is in possession of the basketball. 3 passes the ball out front to Player 1 and then moves toward the top of the key. After receiving the pass from 3, 1 passes quickly to 2 who has cut toward the baseline and then moved in the direction of 1, who assumes a good rebound position. Player 2 immediately makes a pass to 3 at the point area and then moves to pressure the jumper by 3. Under *no* circumstances does 2 block the shot by 3. Player 1 rebounds the shot and gets in the wing line from which the drill originated. The rotation of the other two players occurs as follows: The shooter (3) goes to the opposite wing from which he or she started and the player contesting the shot (2) moves to the end of the line at the top of the key.

Time: A minimum of 3 minutes to a maximum of 10.

Coaching Points: Good drill to use in a pre-game situation. See Appendix A–II, Shooting; Appendix A–V, Passing and Receiving Passes.

FAST-BREAK DRILLS

STRAIGHT-DOWN DRILL
(NO BOUNCE ON FLOOR)

Purpose: Players learn to fill lanes properly on the fast break by the wings staying wide by the sidelines—executing a good sharp cut at the foul line extended and the middle player being under control at the foul line. They will also work on rebounding and outletting the basketball.

Number of Personnel: Minimum of three players to a maximum of eighteen and a coach.

Equipment and Facilities: A full court and at least two basketballs.

Procedure: Players 1 and 3 are the wings (they must stay wide, near the sideline) and 2 is the middle player in a fast break situation (see Diagram 7.1). The drill begins with 2 passing to 1 and receiving a return pass. Player 2 then dribbles to the foul line and makes a pass to 3 cutting to the basket. After making the pass, 2 touches the baseline and fills 3's lane going back down court. Player 1 rebounds 3's shot, then hits 3 with an outlet pass as he or she fills 1's outside lane. Player 3 returns pass to 1 who dribbles to the foul line and then hits 2 for a lay-up. Next three players then step up and execute the drill.

Time: As long as the coach desires.

Coaching Points: Make sure players are executing the drill at maximum speed. See Appendix C-I, Three-Player Fast-Break Rules.

THREE-ON-TWO, TWO-ON-ONE DRILL

Purpose: Offensive and defensive players learn to function in a three-on-two and a two-on-one fast break situation.

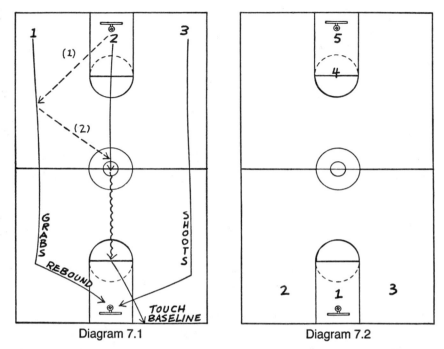

Diagram 7.1   Diagram 7.2

Number of Personnel: Minimum of five players to a maximum of twenty and a coach.

Equipment and Facilities: A full court and at least two basketballs.

Procedure: Players 1, 2, and 3 all rebound a shot from the coach and then begin to fast break and fill the lanes properly (see Diagram 7.2). Middle player on break stops at foul line and stays back on defense. Players 4 and 5 break up court against 1 after gaining possession of the basketball. Other two players (2 and 3) stay down other end of court and play defense. The next three players repeat the process and work on the three-on-two situation. Coach could also make the one defensive player coming back down the court be the first player to shoot the ball in the three-on-two situation.

Time: Time is decided on by the coach.

Coaching Points: Two defensive players should set up in a tandem with top person playing the ball and the back defender playing the first pass. Player at the top drops opposite the direction of the first pass. See Appendix C–I, Three-Player Fast-Break Rules; Appendix C–II, Two-on-One Fast-Break Rules.

THREE-PLAYER WITH CHASER DRILL

Purpose: Offensive players work on three-on-two fast break when the opportunity arises and practice the basic principles of three-on-three basketball as well. Defensive players work on solid defense trying to prevent a quick basket by the offense. Competitive situation increases intensity.

Number of Personnel: A minimum of twelve players to a maximum of twenty and a coach.

Equipment and Facilities: A full court and one basketball.

Procedure: Drill begins as shown in Diagram 7.3 with three members of the white team breaking on a three-on-two situation against two defensive members of the blue team. As soon as the dribbler hits midcourt the next member of the blue team runs and touches the half-court circle and then chases to help out on defense. If the white team does not get the quick fast-break basket, they have to play three-on-three with only one dribble per player. As soon as the blue team gets the ball they break downcourt against two white team defenders who have already positioned themselves in the lane. The three white team members who started the drill return to the end of their team line on the sideline. The drill is set in continuous motion. Can be played to ten or fifteen baskets.

Time: Time will depend upon how long it takes a team to win.

Coaching Points: Two defensive players set up in a tandem with top person

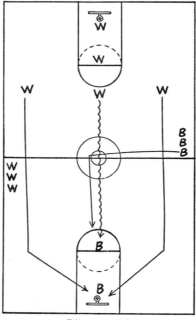

Diagram 7.3

playing the ball and the back defender playing the first pass. See Appendix C–I, Three-Player Fast-Break Rules.

PENN STATE DRILL

Purpose: To teach players the fundamentals of a three-player fast break, rebounding and outletting the basketball, and throwing an accurate baseball pass.

Number of Personnel: A minimum of six players to a limit of eighteen, and a coach.

Equipment and Facilities: A full court and one basketball.

Procedure: Drill begins with three players spread out across a baseline (see Diagram 7.4), and the ball in the hands of a wing player. As the three players proceed upcourt, the wing passes to the middle player who in turn passes ball to the opposite wing. The middle player receives a return pass, dribbles to the foul line, and stops. Middle player can bounce pass to either wing cutting to the basket and then become outlet player on *same* side from which shot is taken. The wing who does not shoot is the rebounder and throws to outlet player. Outlet player then throws a baseball pass down to one of the outside people lined up on the baseline. The next three players then execute the drill.

Time: Coach determines duration of drill.

Coaching Points: Be sure that players execute the drill at maximum performance level. See Appendix C–I, Three-Player Fast-Break Rules; Appendix B–III, Defensive Rebounding.

NEVADA DRILL

Purpose: To instruct players on executing a fast break with five players involved. Also a good conditioning drill.

Number of Personnel: Groups of five.

Equipment and Facilities: A full court and one basketball per five-player group.

Procedure: Player 4 is assigned to get the ball out of the basket after each shot and inbound the ball. Other players touch the baseline after every shot and get to their spots immediately. Their spots are shown in Diagram 7.5. The players continue up and down court for ten consecutive, well-executed baskets The players fill their lanes as shown in the diagram. Player 1 must make sure that each player takes a shot.

Time: Duration of drill will be determined by how long it takes a group to

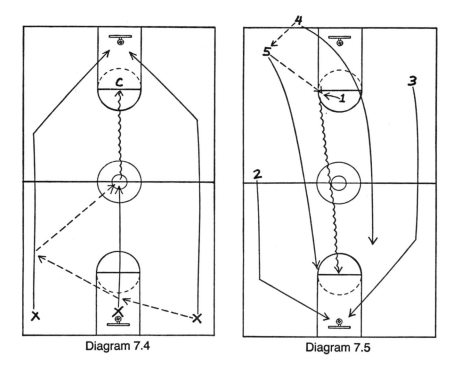

Diagram 7.4   Diagram 7.5

execute ten straight baskets properly. Coach could also set a time limit of 2 to 4 minutes if so desired.

Coaching Points: Players must hustle up and down the floor to get to their spots. See Appendix C–III, Five-Player Fast-Break Rules.

BREAK-FROM-ZONE DRILL

Purpose: Players learn to make strong outlet pass to proper spot, getting the ball into the middle, and filling the lanes on a fast break.

Number of Personnel: Groups of five.

Equipment and Facilities: A full court and a basketball.

Procedure: If rebound goes to a side player (4 or 3), then wing (1 or 2) on his or her side goes out to foul line extended for outlet pass and other wing moves to middle to receive pass. Other players fill the lanes in the manner shown in Diagram 7.6. If ball rebounds to 5, then the coach must designate 1 or 2 to go to the middle for the outlet pass and the other to go to foul line extended on his side. Players then fill lanes for the fast break.

Time: Coach determines the duration of the drill.

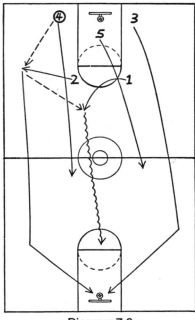

Diagram 7.6

Coaching Points: See Appendix C–III, Five-Player Fast-Break Rules; Appendix B–III, Defensive Rebounding.

START-THE-BREAK DRILL

Purpose: To teach players to fill lanes properly on a fast break from a scramble type situation.

Number of Personnel: Groups of five players and a coach.

Equipment and Facilities: A full court and one basketball.

Procedure: Coach throws ball to one of the five players clustered in a corner of a half court (see Diagram 7.7). The player who gets the ball cannot dribble it to the middle. The other players must fill the lanes with big players acting as trailers and going to the boxes on either side of the lane.

Time: Duration of drill is designated by the coach.

Coaching Points: See Appendix C–III, Five-Player Fast-Break Rules.

DEFENSIVE TRAILER DRILL

Purpose: Offensive players work on quick, proper execution of the three-

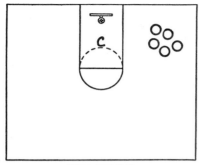

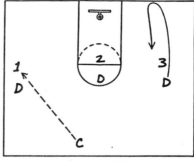

| Diagram 7.7 | Diagram 7.8 |

player break while defensive players hustle back to defensive position and stop a quick score.

Number of Personnel: Groups of six players and a coach.

Equipment and Facilities: A full court and one basketball per group.

Procedure: Coach begins drill by throwing ball to player 1 (see Diagram 7.8). The defensive person on 3 must touch the baseline. Offensive players now break in a three-on-two situation. Defensive trailer must read where the open player is and cover. When coming back down the court, the offensive and defensive players change roles.

Time: Coach runs the drill for as long as he or she desires.

Coaching Points: The two players back on defense initially should set up in a tandem with top person playing the ball and the back player guarding the first pass. Defender on top drops to opposite box after first pass. See Appendix C–I, Three-Player Fast-Break Rules.

FOUL-SHOT, FAST-BREAK DRILL

Purpose: Work on foul shooting and offensive and defensive performance in a three-on-two fast-break situation.

Number of Personnel: Groups of six players.

Equipment and Facilities: A full court and one basketball.

Procedure: One three-player team shoots a foul shot (see Diagram 7.9). The shooter does *not* go back on D. The three defensive players on the lane break off miss-or-make in a three-on-two situation. The teams change roles when coming back down the court. It is also possible for the coach to make this a competitive situation by keeping track of points scored and playing to a total of twenty-five points.

Time: Duration is determined by the coach.

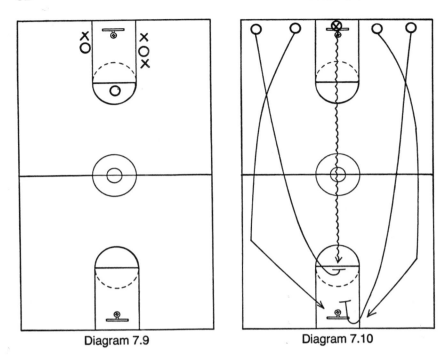

Diagram 7.9   Diagram 7.10

Coaching Points: The two players getting back on defense form a tandem. Top person plays the ball, and the back defender takes the first pass. On the pass, the player at the top drops to box opposite the pass. See Appendix C–I, Three-Player Fast-Break Rules; Appendix A–III, Free-Throw Shooting.

FIVE ACROSS BASELINE—
OUTSIDE PLAYERS ON "D"

Purpose: To teach defensive players to hustle back to play good position defense on three offensive players working on the fast break.

Number of Personnel: Groups of five players and a coach. Up to twenty players can run the drill.

Equipment and Facilities: A full court and a basketball for each group of five players, and a whistle for the coach.

Procedure: The coach begins the drill by lining up five players across the baseline (see Diagram 7.10). There should be a guard in the middle to handle the ball. At the whistle, the outside players sprint to play defense and the ballhandler and two inside players break to score immediately. The coach can run each group of five continuously for a given period or different groups of five one right after another.

Time: Coach determines duration.

Coaching Points: Defensive players establish a tandem in order to prevent the score on the fast break. Top player plays the basketball, and the back defender takes the first pass. Player at the top drops to box opposite the first pass. See Appendix C–I, Three-Player Fast-Break Rules.

ELEVEN-PLAYER
FAST-BREAK DRILL

Purpose: A continuous three-on-two fast-break drill which also stresses conditioning.

Number of Personnel: A minimum of eleven players to a maximum of fifteen and a coach.

Equipment and Facilities: A full court and one basketball.

Procedure: Coach should set up two players on defense and two players in wing positions at each end of floor, in addition to three players going on the break against two of the defensive players (see Diagram 7.11). The one person out of the five who gains control of the basketball goes on the break to the other end of the floor with the two players in the wing positions. The

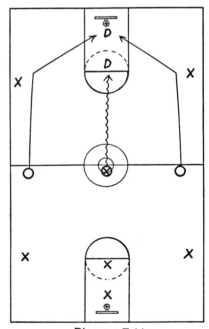

Diagram 7.11

other four players will fill the two defensive spots and the two wings. Drill continues in the same fashion back down the floor.

Time: Duration determined by coach.

Coaching Points: Coach may reward a player for getting involved in four consecutive fast breaks in order to encourage players to give maximum effort at all times. The two defensive players should set up in a tandem. Top person guards the player with the ball while the back defender plays the first pass. Player at the top drops to box opposite the first pass. See Appendix C–I, Three-Player Fast-Break Rules; Appendix B–III, Defensive Rebounding.

THREE-PLAYER STRAIGHT-BREAK DRILL

Purpose: To instruct players on proper techniques of filling the lanes on a fast break. Wings stay wide and make sharp cut to the basket while middle player stops at foul line and makes a good pass to a cutting wing.

Number of Personnel: Minimum of three players to a maximum of eighteen and a coach.

Equipment and Facilities: A full court and at least two basketballs—best if each group of three players has a ball.

Procedure: The drill works on proper fast-break techniques. The coach must make sure the wing players stay wide and plant outside feet at the foul line extended in order to make sharp cut to basket (see Diagram 7.12). The middle player on the break dribbles to foul line and stops, looking to make a good bounce pass to one of the cutting wings. The players could go down court in groups of three or could have same three players come back down court on break to other basket.

Time: Duration is determined by the coach.

Coaching Points: See Appendix C–I, Three-Player Fast-Break Rules.

FIVE-ON-THREE DRILL

Purpose: To teach a five-player team to execute a fast-break offense while being pressured on rebound, at half-court, and by their offensive basket.

Number of Personnel: A minimum of eight players to a maximum of sixteen, and a coach.

Equipment and Facilities: A full court and one basketball.

Procedure: Five offensive players set up in one of the team's offenses on the half-court (see Diagram 7.13). The coach takes a shot. Offensive players

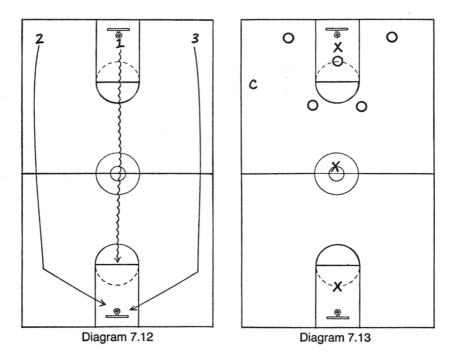

Diagram 7.12   Diagram 7.13

go to their designated rebounding positions. The player who rebounds looks to make strong outlet pass. The one defensive player contests for the rebound and harasses the outlet pass by the rebounder. The middle defensive player contests the ball in the half-court area. The five offensive people are now running the team's fast-break system. When ball gets into the scoring area, the third defensive player contests the ball. Repeat the process as many times as desired by coach. As team becomes more proficient at the drill, the coach can make the defense a two-one-two setup. If the offensive team does not get the original rebound, they must run a ten-second drill.

Time: Coach determines duration.

Coaching Points: The coach must encourage the defensive players to perform their responsibilities with a maximum amount of effort. See Appendix C–III, Five-Player Fast-Break Rules; Appendix B-III, Defensive Rebounding.

FIVE-ON-FIVE RANDOM DRILL

Purpose: To work on a five-on-five fast break while learning defensive positioning, boxing out, rebounding and outletting the basketball. Also, learning to fill lanes on a fast break from various game situations.

Number of Personnel: Ten players perform drill at a time. May need one, two, or three coaches and/or manager.

Equipment and Facilities: A full court and one basketball.

Procedure: One, two, or three coaches and/or managers act as passers during the drill (see Diagram 7.14). Five offensive players freelance. Coaches may either pass ball around the perimeter or take a shot. The five defensive players must react to wherever the ball is passed. They must remember to see both the player they are guarding and the ball, and also keep in mind other sound defensive principles. The drill now operates one of the following four ways:

1. If a coach takes a shot, the defense must block out and get rebound. They then fast break to other end of the floor with the offensive players converting to defense.

2. If a coach passes to the offense, then they try to score. If shot is missed, defense rebounds and fast breaks.

3. One of the coaches may pass to a defensive player, causing a quick fast break.

4. Coach may simply roll ball out on floor to create a loose ball situation and see who comes up with ball. Whoever gains possession simply throws ball back to a coach.

Time: Duration as desired by the coach.

Coaching Points: See Appendix C–III, Five-Player Fast-Break Rules; Appendix B–III, Defensive Rebounding; Appendix C–II, Off-the-Ball Defense.

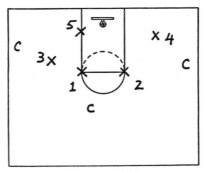

Diagram 7.14

TWO-ON-ONE DRILL

Purpose: Teaching players to run a quick and effective two-on-one fast break.

Number of Personnel: A minimum of eight players to a maximum of sixteen, and a coach.

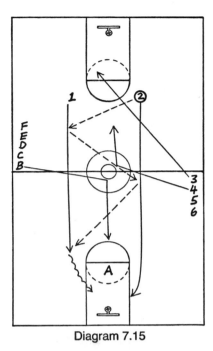

Diagram 7.15

Equipment and Facilities: A full court and one basketball.

Procedure: Players 1 and 2 pass the ball back and forth while breaking against A who is on defense (see Diagram 7.15). They may not dribble the ball until they get in the scoring area. The coach should make sure that 1 and 2 stay about fifteen feet apart. As soon as the ball crosses half-court B sprints and touches the half-court circle and then helps teammate on defense, and Player 3 sprints and becomes defensive player on opposite end of the court. Players 1 and 2 try to score while in the two-on-one situation. If they do not score immediately, then they will be in a two-on-two situation with A and B playing defense. Coach lets them play two-on-two for only ten seconds. After a score, a steal by defense, or a similar event, A and B break two-on-one against 3 on defense. Players 1 and 2 go to the end of their line on the sideline. When ball crosses half-court, 4 touches half-court circle and joins 3 on defense; C sprints and goes to the opposite end for defense. The process is repeated as the drill continues.

Time: Drill is continued either for a time period designated by the coach or until one team gets a designated number of baskets.

Coaching Points: See Appendix C–II, Two-on-One Fast-Break Rules.

PRESS OFFENSE
AND FAST-BREAK DRILL

Purpose: Players work on proper execution of the team's fast-break system and the team's offense versus a full-court press.

Number of Personnel: Players run drill in groups of five, perhaps with two or three groupings of five on the same full court.

Equipment and Facilities: A full court and one basketball.

Procedure: The drill is done on a dummy (no defense) basis. Players rebound a shot and then either run one of the previous fast-break drills to the other end of the court or the team's fast-break system. When a shot is made at the other end of the floor, all five players must run out of bounds and then immediately jump into a full-court press offense and execute it to the opposite end of the floor. The coach may want to designate which player shoots on each trip down the court in the fast-break drill.

Time: Coach determines duration.

Coaching Points: The coach must make sure that players run out of bounds to ensure that all players hustle up and down the court and get to their designated spots on both the fast break and the press offense. When coaching the press offense, be sure that players are looking to pass the ball up the court, are coming to meet each pass, and, when receiving a pass, are turning and looking for someone ahead.

FIVE-ON-THREE
BREAK-COMPETITIVE DRILL

Purpose: Players learn to get quick scoring opportunities against the defense in a fast-break situation. This drill also provides the opportunity for the coach to test the team's fast break system against limited pressure. Team members concentrate on their foul shots because of the competitive nature of the drill.

Number of Personnel: Ten players to perform the drill and a coach or manager to keep score.

Equipment and Facilities: A full court and one basketball.

Procedure: The ten players are divided into two squads. In Diagram 7.16 the two teams are the Blue team (B) and the White team (W). The drill begins with one member of the Blue team shooting a foul shot. If he or she makes the foul shot, then Blue is awarded one point and White gets the ball out of the basket and runs the team's fast-break system to the other end of the court. The two members of the Blue team that are on the foul lane during the free throw contest the outlet pass but do *not* run back to play defense. The White

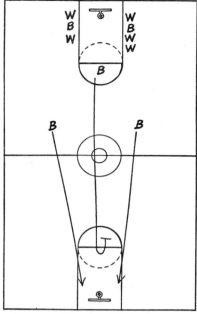

Diagram 7.16

team is therefore executing a five-on-three fast break. If the White team scores a basket or is fouled during their break they are awarded two points. They may also rebound a missed shot in order to score. If the Blue team member misses the original foul shot, the two Blue players on the foul lane try to get an offensive rebound. When they rebound the basketball, they look to score immediately. If they are fouled or score the basket, then their team is awarded two points and a new foul shooter takes a second foul shot and the process is repeated.

After the White squad has completed their fast break they shoot a foul shot. This time the Blue team will run the fast break to the other end of the court. The drill now continues as previously described. Each team must rotate foul shooters, giving each squad member a chance.

Time: The drill continues either for a given time period (5 to 10 minutes) or until one team scores twenty-one points.

Coaching Points: See Appendix C–III, Five-Player Fast-Break Rules; Appendix B–III, Defensive Rebounding; Appendix A–III, Free-Throw Shooting.

FREE-THROW DRILLS

FREE-THROW LADDER

Purpose: To improve player's free-throw shooting percentage by using a competitive situation.

Number of Personnel: The entire team.

Equipment and Facilities: As many baskets as possible and a ball at each basket.

Procedure: The coach places players' names on a poster. To help coach prepare the poster, players pair off and shoot twenty-five free throws each. The coach then writes the names in order with the highest scorer at the top. If there are any ties they can be broken by having players shoot one free throw each. Each day thereafter, players challenge one another in an even-odd pattern—Player 2 vs. Player 1, 3 vs. 4, and the next day 2 vs. 3, 4 vs. 5, 6 vs. 7, etc. The coach then adjusts the positioning of the names on the chart according to the results of the challenges. The coach should reward leaders at certain points throughout the season.

Time: Depends on number of participating players.

Coaching Points: The drill should be done at the end of practice. See Appendix A–III, Free-Throw Shooting.

ONE-AND-ONE FOUL-SHOOTING DRILL

Purpose: Players practice shooting free throws and coping with pressure situations.

Number of Personnel: Entire team.

Equipment and Facilities: As many baskets as possible and a basketball at each.

Procedure: Players split into groups of two or three. A player who makes the first shot takes a second. During drill all activity stops as coach blows whistle periodically and calls out the name of a player standing at the line. The player must shoot one foul shot. If the player makes it, the drill continues as before. If the player misses, everyone runs two laps or two ten-second drills.

Time: Duration is determined by the coach.

Coaching Points: This drill can be done at any time during practice. Ideally, it is better to have players perform the drill after they have just completed a physically strenuous activity. See Appendix A–III, Free-Throw Shooting.

PYRAMID DRILL

Purpose: To improve foul shooting percentages by use of a competitive drill.

Number of Personnel: Entire team.

Equipment and Facilities: As many baskets as possible, and a ball at each.

Procedure: Coach makes up a chart listing players' names in a pyramid. The names should be movable. Any player one or two steps below another player on the pyramid offers a challenge. Each player must accept a challenge each day. The players shoot fifteen foul shots in groups of five. Ties are broken by shooting one foul shot at a time. The winners' names go into the level of the pyramid at the challenge. The coach should reward the top person on the pyramid at given points during the season.

Consecutive 60 Club: Anyone who makes sixty free throws in a row becomes a member. The coach should give a special reward to each player who achieves this feat.

Time: Duration will depend on the number of players doing the drill and number of baskets available.

Coaching Points: It is best to run this drill at the end of practice. See Appendix A–III, Free-Throw Shooting.

WORST SHOOTER DRILL

Purpose: To increase free-throw shooting percentage by rewarding winners.

Number of Personnel: Entire team.

Equipment and Facilities: As many baskets as possible and a basketball at each.

Procedure: The coach divides the team into pairs. One pair member shoots free throws against the other. Each player in each group shoots fifteen times. Ties are broken by shooting one foul shot at a time. The winners go to the showers. The losers must stay and pair up again. The drill will eventually end up with one loser. The coach should run the loser.

Time: Depends on number of participating players.

Coaching Points: See Appendix A–III, Free-Throw Shooting.

SHUFFLE AND FREE-THROW DRILL

Purpose: For players to practice shooting foul shots while fatigued and in a pressure situation.

Number of Personnel: Entire team.

Equipment and Facilities: Drill can be done on one full court if the number of baskets is limited. If there are many baskets, a basketball will be needed at each.

Procedure: Coach can split players into groups of three or four and have them shuffle around the lane area of their basket for 60 seconds. The coach must make sure players keep their arms up in the air during the shuffle. The coach then has one person from each group shoot a foul shot. At least four players should shoot. For each miss, players shuffle for 30 more seconds. The coach could also have players shuffle around the full court and then pick just four to six players to shoot foul shots. If they miss, it costs the team 30 seconds more of shuffling for each miss. The coach continues the drill until either there are no misses or with the last group shooting he or she makes each miss worth a 30-second line drill.

Time: Dependent upon the success of the players.

Coaching Points: The drill is best performed either at the very beginning of practice or at the end. See Appendix A–III, Free-Throw Shooting.

TEAM CONSECUTIVE
FREE-THROW DRILL

Purpose: To increase the accuracy of players' foul shooting by placing them in a competitive situation.

Number of Personnel: Whole team.

Equipment and Facilities: As many baskets as possible and a basketball for each group.

Procedure: The coach divides players into teams of three or four. Each player shoots two free throws at a time and keeps track of how many free throws are made consecutively in a given time period. The team with the highest number of successful free throws in a row wins. The losers have to run. The coach could elect to do drill at the end of practice and let the winners leave and the other teams remain to compete. The last losing team runs at the end.

Time: Determined by coach.

Coaching Points: See Appendix A–III, Free-Throw Shooting,

ONE-AND-ONE AND RUN DRILL

Purpose: For players to practice shooting free throws in a pressure situation.

Number of Personnel: Entire team.

Equipment and Facilities: One basketball and one basket.

Procedure: The coach can pick one, two, three or four players, either during or after practice, to shoot a one-and-one. For each miss the team runs a 10-second drill. If the drill is done at the end of practice, the coach does not let the team leave until players make all the free throws.

Time: Dependent upon the success of the players.

Coaching Points: See Appendix A–III, Free-Throw Shooting.

TEAM FREE-THROW DRILL

Purpose: To improve players' foul shooting by giving them goals to achieve.

Number of Personnel: Entire team.

Equipment and Facilities: One basket and one basketball.

Procedure: To begin drill players all line up around foul line. Each person shoots two foul shots. A coach or manager keeps track of the percentage which is made after everyone on the team has shot twice. The coach should set a goal of 70 percent accuracy for the team for free-throw shooting. The coach must determine what number the players need to make to be closest to that 70 percent. For every one that they are short of the goal, the players run a 10-second drill. After they have run the drills, the players come back to line up around foul lane and shoot again. This time the coach lowers the goal number by one and repeats the process until the players achieve the goal. The goal the players must achieve should never go below 50 percent.

Time: Dependent upon the number of players involved in the drill and how successful the players are at achieving their goals.

Coaching Points: Drill should be done at the end of practice. See Appendix A–III, Free-Throw Shooting.

MAKE-OR-RUN DRILL

Purpose: For players to shoot free throws under the pressure of threat of negative reinforcement.

Number of Personnel: Whole team.

Equipment and Facilities: As many baskets as possible and a basketball at each.

Procedure: The coach divides players up into groups of three or four. They shoot one-and-ones for a given period of time. Players rotate in their group after each one-and-one situation. If a player misses the front end of the one and one, he or she must run two laps around the floor. If player misses the second half of the one-and-one one lap is run. A player who makes both shots does not run.

Time: Coach determines duration.

Coaching Points: Drill can be done at any time during practice. See Appendix A–III, Free-Throw Shooting.

CONSECUTIVE FREE-THROW DRILL

Purpose: Drill gives a goal for players to achieve while shooting free throws.

Number of Personnel: Whole team.

Equipment and Facilities: As many baskets as possible and a basketball at each.

Procedure: The drill is to be done at the end of practice. Coach divides players into groups and tells them they must make a given number of free throws in a row in order to leave. They cannot leave until they make the required number. Each player shoots two free throws at a time.

Time: Depends upon the success of the players.

Coaching Points: See Appendix A–III, Free-Throw Shooting.

ONE-SHOT LEAVE DRILL

Purpose: Players shoot foul shots and are rewarded for making their shots. To improve players' concentration.

Number of Personnel: Whole team.

Equipment and Facilities: One basket, one basketball, and a full court.

Procedure: At the end of practice the coach lines players up on a baseline. One player comes out at a time to shoot one foul shot. If successful, the player then gets to leave. A player who misses goes to the end of the line and the entire team runs a ten-second drill. The coach continues the process until no one is left. Coach could also make it a one-and-one situation.

Time: Depends upon the success of the players.

Coaching Points: See Appendix A–III, Free-Throw Shooting.

PSYCHO-CYBERNETICS
FREE-THROW DRILL

Purpose: For players to practice shooting free throws both physically and mentally. The drill is designed to increase a player's confidence in his or her ability to shoot free throws successfully.

Number of Personnel: One player shoots at a basket at a time. There should be a coach to supervise the players, especially in the early stages of the drill. There should be no more than three players at a basket. The coach may also wish to have a person recording the number of made baskets for each player during the drill.

Equipment and Facilities: The more baskets that are available, the more players who can participate in the drill. One basketball is needed at each basket. If the coach is recording the number of made foul shots for each player, scorekeeping materials will be required.

Procedure: Poor foul shooting is often a player's psychological problem. Players with excellent shooting form often have trouble shooting free throws successfully. Sometimes they are good foul shooters but have periodic slumps during the season. This is often due to a lack of confidence. Players tense up at the foul line rather than feeling relaxed and confident. This drill is designed to help players build up their self-confidence by using successful mental rehearsal techniques. The drill is done in five stages. Each step is clearly explained below.

1. Players shoot five foul shots physically. They relax and have confidence while shooting.

2. With their eyes open, players now shoot five foul shots mentally. They go through the motions of shooting the foul shot without using a basketball, vividly imaging that each shot attempted is successful, picturing the basketball going through the hoop on each attempt.

3. With their eyes closed, players mentally shoot five more free throws.

This time they do not go through the actual motions of shooting the basketball. They should be standing at the foul line and visualizing themselves shooting five successful foul shots. Again, they must be able to see themselves making each foul shot.

4. In this stage, players close their eyes and shoot five foul shots both mentally and physically. They actually shoot a basketball in this stage, picturing themselves as they did in Step 3.

5. In the final stage, the players once again shoot five free throws physically with their eyes open. Again, they must relax and have confidence while shooting.

Note: During the drill, players are not to worry about making mistakes. They should not be overly concerned with the outcome of each foul shot. They are to concentrate only on imagining that each free throw attempted is successful. They should "see" the ball go in the basket prior to each time they shoot.

Time: Depends on the number of players involved and the number of baskets available.

Coaching Points: The drill can be done at any time during practice. The coach must make sure that there is absolute silence for maximum concentration. See Appendix A–III, Free-Throw Shooting.

INSIDE MOVES

INSIDE-MOVE DRILL

Purpose: Offensive players learn post-up techniques and moves for scoring when receiving the pass inside. Defensive players practice solid defense on post player.

Number of Personnel: Minimum of four players to a maximum of eight per basket and a coach.

Equipment and Facilities: One basket for every four to eight players and two basketballs per basket.

Procedure: Coach instructs offensive player to take position on the foul lane to receive a pass (see Diagram 9.1). The offensive post player must be on the box or above it. The offensive player must get into the habit of looking over the baseline shoulder right after receiving the ball, and then moving to the basket. Sample moves include the inside power move, hook shot, turn

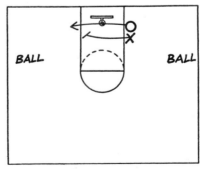

Diagram 9.1

around-jump shot, pivot-turn and face the defensive player then take player to the hole. Defense works on defending the post. Each player in the two wing positions is to have a basketball. They look to make pass into the post. As soon as the post players complete the drill on one side of the lane they move to the other side for pass from opposite wing.

Time: Coach determines duration.

Coaching Points: See Appendix A-IV, Inside Moves; Appendix B-II, Off-the-Ball Defense.

MIKAN DRILLS

Purpose: Players practice the following skills: right-and left-handed lay-up, right- and left-handed hook shot, power move, and ball fake then power move. Also a good conditioning drill.

Number of Personnel: One or two players per basketball and possibly a timekeeper.

Equipment and Facilities: One basket and a basketball for every two players and, if running drill for a specific time period, a stopwatch.

Procedure:

Drill #1: Right and Left Hand Lay-Ups. Player stands to the right of the basket *inside* the foul lane area at Point A (see Diagram 9.2). Drill begins with player taking a right-handed lay-up, catching ball before it hits the floor, and executing a left-handed lay-up from the left side of the basket at Point B. Goal should be either to make twenty-five baskets in a row without stopping or to do the drill for one minute.

Drill #2: Hook Shot. Do the same as in (1) only the player uses a right-handed and left-handed hook instead of a layup. Goal is the same as in (1), as well.

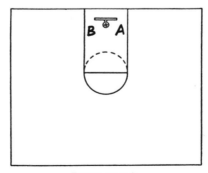

Diagram 9.2

Drill #3: Power Move. Player stands to the right of the basket at Point A with shoulders and feet parallel to the baseline. While jumping up to the basket, player must execute a strong power move so that even if closely guarded player can get a three-point play. If he or she is a right-handed player, the key is to have the left elbow extended to protect the ball. Player catches ball before it hits the floor and executes the same power move from the left side of the basket, using the right hand as the shooting hand. Left-handed shooters use the left hand in this drill. Goal is the same as in (1) and (2).

Drill # 4: Head and Ball Fake. Player follows the same procedure as in (3) but uses a head and ball fake before shooting, remembering to show the ball during the fake. In other words, player brings the ball out of the chest on a 45° angle and up to about eye level during fake. Then player jumps in toward basket for a three-point play. Goal should be the same as in earlier drills. Coach must make sure player uses proper form in executing the ball fake.

Time: Each player executes each of the four drills for 1 minute or until the player has made twenty-five successful shots in a row.

Coaching Points: Coach must encourage players to perform drill at maximum effort. For drills 1 and 2 see Appendix A-II, Shooting; for Drills 3 and 4 see Appendix A-IV, Inside Moves.

POWER-MOVE DRILL

Purpose: For conditioning, and practice for a good power move.

Number of Personnel: Two to four players per basket and a timekeeper.

Equipment and Facilities: Two basketballs per basket, enough baskets for participating players, and a stopwatch.

Procedure: Coach should place a ball on either box on each side of lane (see Diagram 9.3). Player M has back to the basketballs while standing in

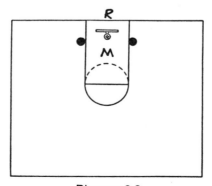

Diagram 9.3

the middle of the lane. Player R yells "Go" and M gets one ball and power moves up to the basket. R rebounds the shot and places the ball back on box as quickly as possible. M then gets the other ball and does a power move from that side of the basket. Players continue the process for the duration of the drill.

Time: Each player executes drill for 30 to 60 seconds.

Coaching Points: Coach should establish a goal for players to achieve while performing the drill. See Appendix A–IV, Inside Moves.

BIG PLAYER DRILLS

Purpose: To teach players the proper footwork and a variety of offensive moves that can be used when getting the basketball on the inside.

Number of Personnel: One to six players per basket and a coach.

Equipment and Facilities: A basketball per basket and as many baskets as necessary to accommodate participating players.

Procedure: There are two ways to begin these drills: (1) Players stand in the lane, spin ball out in front of them, and then jump and land on both feet so that they may use either foot as a pivot foot, or (2) players line up away from coach, who has a basketball. Players move toward a designated spot in order to receive a pass from the coach. Players should receive the ball in good form: jump stop, feet square and *wide,* knees flexed, rear out, hands cupped and ready for pass. They must always receive the pass above the box on the foul lane, and also give a target to the passer.

Drill #1: Player takes one giant step from underneath the basket out toward the middle of the lane, with back to the basket. He or she spins the ball out to the left, goes to get it, and drops left foot toward the basket and then executes a hook shot. Proper form for a hook: Player puts ball and one hand on thigh and the other hand on top of ball, drops foot toward the basket and looks over shoulder in order to arch back. Player then drives leg *up* as if in a high jump. The target for the shot should be the box on the backboard. Player must make sure to get the rebound before the ball hits the floor.

Drill #2: Player does the same drill as above, but spins the ball to the right. *Note:* With Drills 1 and 2, a player on either side of the basket can work on both right- and left-handed hook just by switching which foot is dropped toward the basket.

Drill #3: Player starts at the top of the foul line and goes to the right, takes one dribble, then two steps, and makes a hook shot. Player should use a crossover step for the initial move to the hoop and head for the box on the lane.

Drill #4: Player does the same as above, but moves to the left.

Drill #5: Player goes to the right side of the lane and spins the ball out, catching the ball with back to the basket. Player then pivots on baseline foot and keeps the ball up in the chin area, examines defense and takes a jump shot.

Drill #6: Player does the same as above on the left side of the basket.

Drill #7: On right side of the basket, the player does the same as in Drill 5 except instead of taking a jump shot, he or she does a crossover step, takes one dribble, then two steps, and a hook shot. Remember: On the drive the player should go for the box on the other side of the lane.

Drill #8: Player does the same as in Drill 7 except from the left side.

Drill #9: Player does the same as in Drill 5 but pivots on foot nearest the foul line.

Drill #10: Player does the same as above but on the left side of the lane.

Drill #11: Player does the same as in Drill 9 except instead of taking a jump shot, does a crossover step, takes one dribble and two steps (after last step feet should be parallel with the backboard). Now, he or she executes a ball fake by bringing the ball out of the chest (but not taking ball over head) and powers the ball up to basket on the shot.

Drill #12: Player does the same as in Drill 11 except from the left side.

Drill #13: Player gets the ball on the box or above it on left hand side of the lane, then looks over the baseline (right) shoulder and drops right foot directly toward the basket. Player takes one dribble and two steps (after last step feet should be parallel with the backboard), and executes a ball fake by bringing the ball out of the chest (but not taking ball over head) and powers the ball up to the basket on the shot.

Drill #14: Player does the same as in Drill 13 except from the right side of lane. Remember, this time left foot will be dropped toward the basket.

Drill #15: Player goes to the box or above it on left-hand side of the foul lane, looking over baseline (right) shoulder but dropping the left foot across the lane. After taking one dribble and two steps, player makes a baby hook shot.

Drill #16: Same as Drill 15 except player starts on the right-hand side of the foul lane. This time player looks over left shoulder but drops the right foot across the lane.

Drill #17: Same as in Drill 15 except player fakes the drop step across the lane with left foot, pivots on right foot, squares up for a jumper, and goes straight up for the shot. Player must not fade away on the shot.

Drill #18: Same as in Drill 17 except from the right side of the lane. That means player will fake the drop step across the lane with the right foot and pivot back on left foot in order to take the jump turn around jump shot.

Time: Depends on how many drills the coach wants to do during practice. Should not spend more than 15 minutes on the drills.

Coaching Points: Coach must emphasize to players the need to execute the proper footwork associated with each of the moves described. Drills are designed to work on technique. See Appendix A–IV, Inside Moves; Appendix A–II, Shooting.

POSTING-UP DRILL

Purpose: Offensive inside players work on positioning around the lane and making proper moves when receiving a pass. Offensive perimeter players learn to make good passes to the post players. Defensive players try to front post player and make it difficult for the offensive perimeter players to pass the ball inside.

Number of Personnel: A minimum of five players to a maximum of eight per basket and a coach.

Equipment and Facilities: One basketball at each basket.

Procedure: The three perimeter players look to make a pass (no lob passes are allowed) to the inside player (see Diagram 9.4). The inside offensive player works to get position as the ball is passed around the perimeter. Once he or she receives a pass inside, player must execute a proper move against the defensive player. The coach can decide to run the drill first with no defense guarding the perimeter players and can later add defensive players on them to contest passes inside. The defensive players guarding the perimeter players should let them pass the ball around freely, but contest whoever has the ball. This is also a good defensive drill for working on fronting the post.

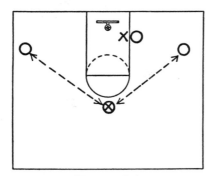

Diagram 9.4

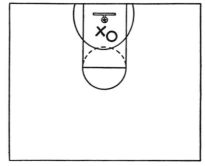

Diagram 9.5

Time: Depends on the number of participating players. Generally 5 to 10 minutes will be adequate.

Coaching Points: Coach must observe the inside offensive player's work, the defender's work, and the passers' abilities to get the ball inside. See Appendix A–IV, Inside Moves; Appendix A–V, Passing and Receiving Passes; Appendix B–II, Off-the-Ball Defense.

NO FOUL, NO JUMP BALL DRILL

Purpose: Players learn to make strong moves around the basket area with a player hanging on them in a competitive situation.

Number of Personnel: Minimum of two players to a maximum of eight per basket and a coach.

Equipment and Facilities: A basketball for each pair of players and as many baskets as possible.

Procedure: Players of about equal size pair up at basket. They play one-on-one under the basket, keeping ball in the area shown in Diagram 9.5. There are no fouls or jump balls in this drill. The first player to reach ten baskets wins. Losers run a 30-second line drill.

Time: Time will be determined by how long it takes a player to make ten baskets.

Coaching Points: Coach must make sure that the players do not get carried away and use excessive physical contact. See Appendix A–IV, Inside Moves; Appendix A–VII, Offensive Rebounding; Appendix B–III, Defensive Rebounding.

PICK-UP DRILL

Purpose: To teach players to react quickly to take a shot; to be quick but not hurried.

Number of Personnel: One to six players per basket and a coach.

Equipment and Facilities: One basketball and as many baskets as needed for the number of players.

Procedure: Player stands underneath the basket with back to the coach (see Diagram 9.6). Coach rolls the ball on the floor and yells, "Ball." Player turns quickly and hustles after the basketball. Just before player reaches the ball, coach yells either "Jumper" or "Lay-up." When the player picks up the basketball, he or she must execute whatever shot the coach called. Drill should be used mostly for the taller players.

Time: Duration determined by coach.

Coaching Points: Coach must be sure to keep the player working hard for a given time period. See Appendix A–II, Shooting.

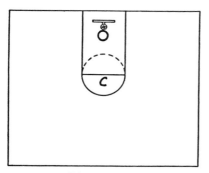

Diagram 9.6

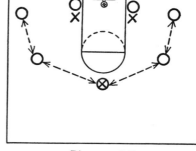

Diagram 9.7

POST DRILL

Purpose: Offensive players learn to work together to get open for receiving pass inside and making proper inside move. Defensive players work to prevent ball from getting inside.

Number of Personnel: Minimum of eight players to a maximum of fourteen and a coach.

Equipment and Facilities: One basketball and a half court.

Procedure: The coach places an offensive post player on each box and defensive players against them (see Diagram 9.7). Coach also places four or five other players around the perimeter. The players on the perimeter pass the ball around and look to make good pass inside. They work on passing to the post players. Post players concentrate on their inside moves and working together by setting screens and so forth. They may not go past the foul line. Defensive players try to prevent pass from getting inside.

Time: Coach determines duration.

Coaching Points: The coach has a difficult job in that the inside offensive players, inside defenders, and the perimeter passers must all be observed to see if they are doing their jobs properly. See Appendix A–IV, Inside Moves; Appendix A–V, Passing and Receiving Passes; Appendix A–VIII, Setting and Using Screens; Appendix B–II, Off-the-Ball Defense.

OFFENSIVE-REBOUND-AND-IN DRILL

Purpose: To instruct players on proper method of getting an offensive rebound and then putting the ball in the basket.

Number of Personnel: At least three players, a coach, and a timer at each basket.

Equipment and Facilities: Number of baskets will be determined by the number of participating players. Two basketballs per basket and at least one stopwatch will be needed.

Procedure: Player P should be one of the taller players on the team. The coach begins the drill with two basketballs, throwing one ball up against backboard (see Diagram 9.8). Player P rebounds the shot and puts it back in the basket. As soon as the first ball goes in the coach throws the second ball against the backboard and Player P repeats the process. Two players are stationed underneath the basket so that as soon as shot goes in they can get the ball and toss it back out to the coach.

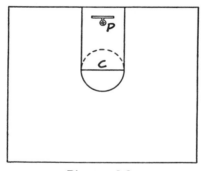

Diagram 9.8

Time: 30 to 60 seconds per player.

Coaching Points: Push player to perform at maximum efficiency. See Appendix A–VII, Offensive Rebounding.

LAY-UP DRILLS

LaSALLE DRIVE
AND JUMP-SHOT SERIES

Purpose: Players work on lay-up skills, shooting a jump shot off the dribble, and the speed, crossover, and hockey step dribbles.

Number of Personnel: Minimum of six players to a maximum of twenty.

Equipment and Facilities: A half court and at least two basketballs.

Procedure: Drill begins by setting up two lines and one player in the outlet spot as shown in Diagram 10.1. The shooting and rebounding lines should be at half-court. Players in the shooting line go hard to the basket using the six moves described below. Players in the rebound line rebound the shot and throw a good outlet pass to the outlet player. The outlet player then passes the ball back out to end of the shooting line, rebounder becomes the new outlet player, and the outlet player goes to the end of the shot line. The six moves are as follows:

1. Players drive hard to the hoop for a lay-up from the right side using a speed dribble.

2. Players drive for a lay-up from the right side and execute a crossover dribble by going toward corner and then crossing over.

3. Players drive to the hoop for a lay-up from the left side using a speed dribble. The outlet player will now be in opposite corner, and the rebound and shot lines switch sides.

4. Players do the same as in (3) except they use a crossover dribble on the drive to the hoop.

5. The shooter drives hard to foul line and takes a good, on-balance jump shot.

6. Players drive to foul line and execute a hockey-step dribble by coming to a stop, banging the feet and shaking head from side to side. They then take one dribble to either side and shoot a jumper.

Time: Coach determines duration.

Coaching Points: This drill is an excellent drill to be used in pre-game warm-up. Coach must encourage players to go through drill at full speed and keep shooting and rebound lines back by half-court. See Appendix A–II, Shooting; Appendix B–III, Defensive Rebounding; Appendix A–I, Ball Handling.

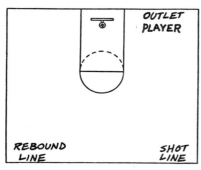
Diagram 10.1

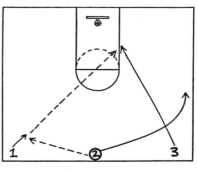
Diagram 10.2

LAY-UP DRILL

Purpose: Players learn lay-up and passing skills.

Number of Personnel: A minimum of six players to a maximum of twenty.

Equipment and Facilities: A half court and at least two basketballs.

Procedure: Player 2 passes to Player 1, then goes to foul line extended on opposite side of the court (see Diagram 10.2). 3 receives pass from 1 and shoots a lay-up, which 1 rebounds. The next time 2 gets pass from 1 and shoots, and 3 rebounds. As soon as 1 passes to 2, 1 goes to opposite foul line extended. Final time—3 passes to 1, 1 shoots, and 2 rebounds. Each player shoots one lay-up before their group of three goes to the end of different lines.

Time: Coach sets time limit.

Coaching Points: Encourage players to perform drill at maximum effort. See Appendix A–II, Shooting.

TWO-BALL WARM-UP DRILL

Purpose: Post players work on ball handling while other players practice cuts to the basket and lay-ups.

Number of Personnel: A minimum of six players to a maximum of twenty.

Equipment and Facilities: Four to six basketballs and a half court.

Procedure: Players A and B set up on each side of the high post (see Diagram 10.3). Other players form two lines out front near half court. Players 1 and 2 begin drill by dribbling left and right respectively and passing into the post player on their side. After the pass each player cuts through the lane, with the player on the left going first. Post players pass to players cutting to the basket for a lay-up. Coach should switch post players after a period of time.

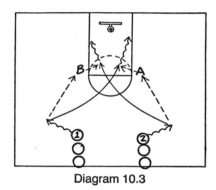

Diagram 10.3

Time: Duration determined by coach.

Coaching Points: Coach should emphasize making good, hard cuts to the basket after passing to the man in the high post. See Appendix A–II, Shooting.

TWENTY-ONE LAY-UPS DRILL

Purpose: Players improve their speed dribble and lay-up in a competitive situation. A good conditioning drill.

Number of Personnel: From two to five players per team, and two teams— one at each basket on a full court. Coach must oversee drill.

Equipment and Facilities: One basketball per team and the number of full courts necessary for each player to participate in the drill.

Procedure: Players work on full-court lay-ups. Players are split into two teams per full court. The first team to make twenty-one lay-ups wins. The

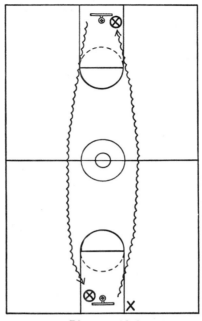

Diagram 10.4

first person in each line on a full-court makes a lay-up at the basket and then speed dribbles down court and back, shooting a lay-up at each end (see Diagram 10.4). All other players on a team speed dribble down court to make lay-up and then shoot a lay-up coming back. Players must succeed in the lay-up at each basket. The coach should have the losers run in this competitive drill.

Time: Drill continues until one team makes a total of twenty-one lay-ups.

Coaching Points: This is an excellent drill to be incorporated in the early season practice plans. Helps to condition athletes while at the same time making it fun for the players because of the competitive nature of the drill. See Appendix A–II, Shooting; Appendix A–I, Ball Handling.

TWENTY-ONE LAY-UPS
WITH OUTLET DRILL

Purpose: Players work on passing and lay-up skills in a competitive setting. Drill is good for conditioning.

Number of Personnel: A minimum of five to a maximum of eight players per team and a coach.

Equipment and Facilities: One basketball per team and as many full courts as necessary for each player to participate in the drill.

Procedure: Drill starts with outlet players in the two spots indicated in Diagram 10.5. The first player in each team's line makes a lay-up at that end. The outlet player throws a baseball pass to the second passer, while the shooter runs to the other end of the court. The last passer gets rebound and throws a long outlet to same shooter going down to the original basket. The rebounder follows the shooter down court and gets in line with their team. A new outlet player then comes out from the line, and the old first outlet player replaces the second passer. The next shooter must be ready to go, rebounds the first shooter's lay-up, and immediately throws outlet pass and sprints down court.

Time: Drill continues until one team makes a total of twenty-one lay-ups.

Coaching Points: Another excellent drill for the early season practice. Good for conditioning while making it exciting for players through competition. Players are also working on a variety of skills: passing, catching, dribbling, and shooting lay-ups at full speed. See Appendix A–II, Shooting; Appendix A–V, Passing and Receiving Passes; Appendix A–I, Ball Handling.

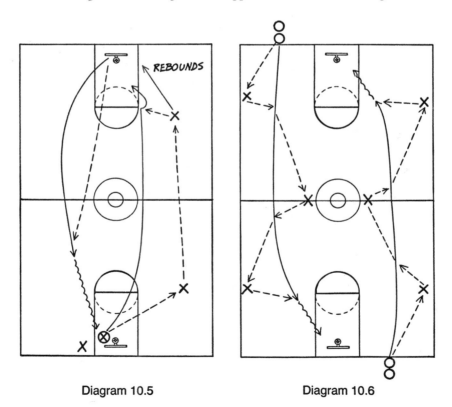

Diagram 10.5   Diagram 10.6

CONTINUOUS LAY-UP DRILL

Purpose: Players practice passing and lay-up skills while working on conditioning.

Number of Personnel: A minimum of twelve players to a maximum of eighteen.

Equipment and Facilities: A full court and at least six basketballs.

Procedure: The drill is set up with six players as passers (x) and a given number of players as shooters (o) (see Diagram 10.6). Each shooter should have a basketball. The passers pass the ball up court while the shooter runs to the basket. Each shooter keeps going until a designated amount of time has elapsed, and players switch roles. The coach can also change from right side to left side.

Time: Duration is decided by coach.

Coaching Points: Drill is designed to be used during the early season portion of practice. Can make the drill into a competitive drill if the squad can be divided into two full-courts competing against one another. See Appendix A–II, Shooting; Appendix A–V, Passing and Receiving Passes.

FOUR-PLAYER-WEAVE
LAY-UP DRILL

Purpose: Players learn to handle the basketball and shoot lay-ups in a good warm-up drill.

Number of Personnel: A minimum of eight players to a maximum of sixteen.

Equipment and Facilities: A half court and at least two basketballs.

Procedure: One of the players at the top of the key passes the ball down to the player on his or her side at the foul line extended and gets a return pass. He or she then hands off on the outside to the other player up top to begin the weave (see Diagram 10.7). Players should always go to the inside when handing off and to the outside when receiving the handoff. The weave should continue for a period of time, after which one of the players goes to the basket with others following.

Time: Coach determines duration.

Coaching Points: Good drill to be used in a pre-game warm-up situation. Players are getting use to handling the basketball while loosening up. See Appendix A–II, Shooting.

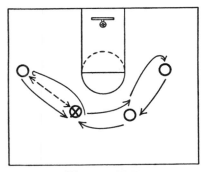

Diagram 10.7

LAY-UP CONTEST WITH PASSERS DRILL

Purpose: Players learn proper passing and lay-up skills in a competitive situation.

Number of Personnel: Four or five players per team and a coach.

Equipment and Facilities: One basketball and a full court per team.

Procedure: The first shooter for each team makes a lay-up and throws pass

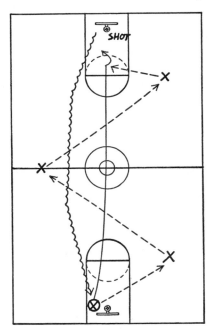

Diagram 10.8

out to a teammate (see Diagram 10.8). Three teammates pass ball to each other to the opposite end of the court where the shooter has sprinted and makes a second lay-up. The shooter then speed dribbles the length of floor to shoot a lay-up. The first team to make a lay-up wins. The shooter is rotated each time the drill is executed. The losers should be made to run.

Time: Drill continues until one team has won a total of five times.

Coaching Points: Excellent drill for use during early season practices. The drill is very good for conditioning players in a competitive situation. See Appendix A–II, Shooting; Appendix A–I, Ball Handling; Appendix A–V, Passing and Receiving Passes.

DRIVE BASELINE, JUMP-STOP LAY-UP DRILL

Purpose: To teach players the proper technique of coming to a two-footed stop before shooting a lay-up.

Number of Personnel: From two to five players per half court.

Equipment and Facilities: At least one basketball and a half court per group of players.

Procedure: The first player in line starts in a corner and drives hard to the basket (see Diagram 10.9). He or she must make a good jump stop to shoot a lay-up and then rebound the ball to pass it to the next player in line. After making lay-up, player goes to the other corner, and each player repeats that process.

Time: Coach determines duration.

Coaching Points: Be sure the players come to a two-footed stop, on balance, with shoulders parallel to the backboard. See Appendix A–II, Shooting.

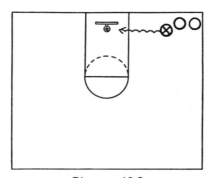

Diagram 10.9

DRIVE FROM FOUL LINE,
JUMP STOP DRILL

Purpose: To instruct players on the proper technique of coming to a jump stop before shooting a lay-up.

Number of Personnel: Two to five players per half court.

Equipment and Facilities: At least one basketball and a half court per group of players.

Procedure: The first player in line drives to the basket from one corner of the foul line and makes a good jump stop before shooting the lay-up (see Diagram 10.10). The shooter then rebounds own shot and passes the basketball out to the next player in line. After passing the ball out, shooter goes to the opposite corner of the foul line. Other players repeat the same process.

Time: Duration determined by coach.

Coaching Points: Players must come to a two-footed stop on balance before shooting. See Appendix A-II, Shooting.

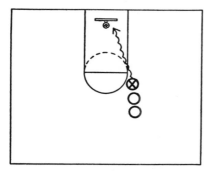

Diagram 10.10

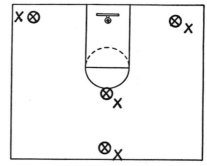

Diagram 10.11

PLAYER-ON-BACK LAY-UP DRILL

Purpose: Players practice shooting lay-ups with a player harassing them from the rear.

Number of Personnel: A minimum of four to a maximum of twelve players per half court and a coach.

Equipment and Facilities: At least two basketballs and a half court.

Procedure: The coach may decide to run the drill from any or all of the four spots indicated in Diagram 10.11. Defensive players start one step behind offensive player with the ball. The offensive players going from the baseline or the top of key should be able to make a lay-up in one dribble. The coach could also have the players work on their jump stops if that is desired. The offensive player coming from midcourt should be able to make a lay-up in two dribbles. Defensive players must contest each shot from behind.

Time: Coach determines duration.

Coaching Points: Coach must emphasize to players the need to concentrate when shooting a lay-up while being contested. They must not turn their head away to worry about a possible block by the defense. See Appendix A–II, Shooting; Appendix A–I, Ball Handling.

CONTESTED LAY-UP DRILL

Purpose: Players learn to shoot lay-up strongly to prevent block.

Number of Personnel: A minimum of four to a maximum of sixteen players per half court and a coach.

Equipment and Facilities: At least two basketballs and a half court.

Procedure: The offensive line starts at top of the key (see Diagram 10.12). Defensive line starts at foul line extended about one step in from the sideline. Coach should work defensive players from both sides of the court. At the coach's whistle, the offensive player drives to the basket while the defensive player hustles to contest the shot. Players then go to the end of the opposite lines. The coach could have offensive players run a 10-second drill if they do not make the lay-up or draw a foul. The coach should make sure that defensive players are going for the block with their inside hand.

Time: Coach decides duration.

Coaching Points: Players must concentrate on a spot and not worry about block when going up for the shot. Offensive people can also work on jump stops. See Appendix A–II, Shooting; Appendix A–I, Ball Handling.

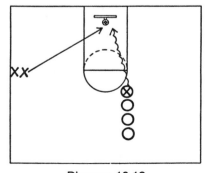

Diagram 10.12

STAR LAY-UP DRILL

Purpose: Players practice passing and lay-up skills.

Number of Personnel: A minimum of six players to a maximum of fifteen.

Equipment and Facilities: A half court and at least two basketballs.

Procedure: Five players start out on the court as shown in Diagram 10.13. The remaining players line up behind the player with the basketball. The next player in line should also have a basketball. After a player makes the pass indicated in the diagram, he or she follows the pass and assumes that spot. Eventually each player will be in all five spots. Note: The player out front by the top of the key is the shooter. He or she should cut to the basket to receive pass, shoot a lay-up without using a dribble, rebound own shot, and then give ball to next player in line without a basketball and go to the end of the line.

Time: Coach determines duration.

Coaching Points: Drill should be used primarily for pre-game warm-up. See Appendix A–II, Shooting; Appendix A–V, Passing and Receiving Passes.

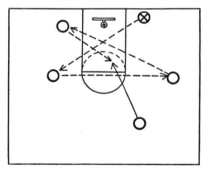

Diagram 10.13

TWO-POST LAY-UP DRILL

Purpose: For players to improve their right- and left-handed lay-ups, and to work on the following passing skills: making accurate passes while moving at top speed and bounce passing to cutters to the basket. Also an excellent conditioning drill.

Number of Personnel: From ten to fourteen players and a coach or manager at each basket to count successful shots.

Equipment and Facilities: A full court for every ten to fourteen players, a watch and a whistle, and two basketballs per full court.

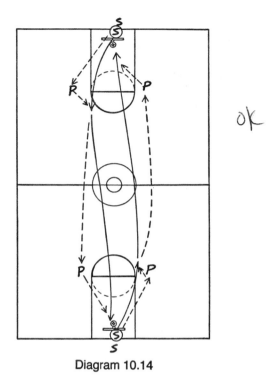

Diagram 10.14

Procedure: Coach places one player at each corner of the foul lines of a full court (designated as P in Diagram 10.14). The players who will be shooting the lay-ups are divided evenly under each basket (S in the diagram). The coach instructs players to shoot the lay-ups from either the left or the right.

At the whistle by the coach, players begin the drill. The first shooters in line at each basket shoot a lay-up at their basket and pass the ball out to the post player nearest them on the appropriate side. The shooters then sprint to the other basket and receive a return chest pass from the post player. The shooters then make a long pass to the post player on the same side of the other basket. The second post player now makes a bounce pass to the shooter cutting to the basket, who makes a lay-up. As soon as the shot goes through the basket, the next shooter comes from underneath the basket, gets the basketball, quickly passes out to the post player nearest them on the appropriate side and repeats the process. The drill is now run continuously.

During the course of the drill, shooters periodically relieve post players of their duties. This way all players get an opportunity to shoot and to be a post player. Players are not allowed to follow up missed lay-ups. If the drill is done using two full courts at the same time, then the two groups should compete against one another. The group that makes the lesser number of lay-ups must run a 30-second line drill.

Time: From 2 to 5 minutes. Players should be able to make twenty lay-ups for the full court for each minute the drill is performed. Example: If the drill is done for two minutes, then there should be forty lay-ups made on the full-court. If for 4 minutes, then eighty successful lay-ups. If only one group is performing the drill, the coach may wish to instruct players that any missed lay-up in the given time period will result in players doing the drill again.

Coaching Points: Drill can be used at any time during the season but is best suited for use in the early season. Players are working on their conditioning while trying to attain a set goal or in a competitive situation. See Appendix A–II, Shooting; Appendix A–V, Passing and Receiving Passes.

PASSING DRILLS

PASSING-UNDER-PRESSURE DRILL

Purpose: Players learn to stay active and pass while under pressure. Offensive players underneath work on power move to the basket.

Number of Personnel: Minimum of four players to a maximum of twelve and a coach.

Equipment and Facilities: At least one basketball and a half court.

Procedure: Drill begins with an offensive player dribbling from half-court at a defensive player stationed at the foul line (see Diagram 11.1). Player X out front stops ball, then covers the player with the basketball. The offensive player with the ball passes only when the coach yells "Pass." He or she has to keep active by pivoting until that time. The low players are on the boxes. The person down low who does not receive the pass covers the other low player as soon as the pass is made. The offensive player down low must then

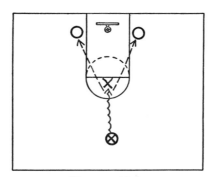

Diagram 11.1

make a good power move to the basket. Coach could also call "Left" or "Right" and have passer make a good pass to the proper low player. Drill could be varied by adding another defensive player on ball at beginning of drill.

Time: 5 to 10 minutes.

Coaching Points: Coach must make sure that the passer does not turn his back to the players stationed on each box. Player must be strong with the ball and keep it moving so as to keep the defender from knocking it away. See Appendix A–V, Passing and Receiving Passes; Appendix B–I, On-the-Ball Defense; Appendix A–IV, Inside Moves.

BREAK THE DOUBLE-TEAM DRILL

Purpose: To teach offensive players to break double-team pressure. Offensive player by basket works on inside moves. Defensive players execute proper double-team techniques and defense against a post player.

Number of Personnel: A minimum of five players to a maximum of twelve and a coach.

Equipment and Facilities: At least one basketball and a half court.

Procedure: Player 1 is given the ball by the coach and is immediately double teamed (see Diagram 11.2). When coach yells "Pass," Player 1 throws to 2 in the low post. As soon as pass is made to 2, X3 moves to cover 2. 2 now makes a strong inside move against X3. The coach must make sure that 1 keeps the ball active and tries to split the defensive players who are double teaming. The drill should be run on both sides of the court.

Time: 5 to 10 minutes.

Coaching Points: Another helpful hint in coaching a man being double teamed is to instruct him to take the ball down. Try to get the defensive

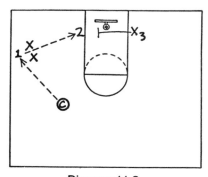

Diagram 11.2

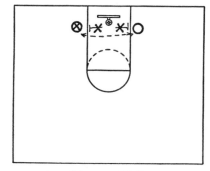

Diagram 11.3

players to lower their hands so that the ball can be passed over top of the hands. See Appendix A–V, Passing and Receiving Passes; Appendix B–I, On-the-Ball Defense; Appendix A–IV, Inside Moves.

PASSING DRILL

Purpose: To teach players to fake and make passes around a defensive player.

Number of Personnel: Any multiple of three players and a coach.

Equipment and Facilities: A basketball for each group of three players. The more players there are that must perform the drill, the more space is needed, but a half court should be sufficient.

Procedure: This drill has no shooting, just passing. Coach should have two players on the boxes passing a basketball back and forth to one another with a defensive player in the middle (see Diagram 11.3). If defender touches the ball, passer goes into the middle. Defensive player must follow the ball as it is passed back and forth and should try to stay within three feet of the basketball at all times.

Time: Approximately 5 minutes.

Coaching Points: Coach must encourage player in the middle to give maximum effort. Offensive players should work on faking passes. See Appendix A–V, Passing and Receiving Passes.

THREE-IN-THE-RING DRILL

Purpose: Offensive players work on passing under double-team pressure while defensive players learn double-teaming techniques and anticipating where a pass is going to be made.

Number of Personnel: Ten to twelve players and a coach.

Equipment and Facilities: One basketball and a half court.

Procedure: The drill starts with the coach passing a ball to one of the players in the circle (see Diagram 11.4). The two players in the middle (11 and 12) are closest to the ball and go to double team the ball. Player 1 then tries to pass to anyone on the circle except for the two players on either side (2 and 9). Player 10 is the third defensive player and tries to intercept the pass. If 10 intercepts the pass or gets a hand on it, he or she replaces 1 on the circle, and 1 goes into the middle.

Time: 5 to 10 minutes.

Coaching Points: Coach must make sure that no lob passes are thrown. Player being double teamed should try to keep ball down in order to lower the defenders' hands, try to step through the pressure, and stay active with the ball so as to prevent from being tied up into a held ball situation. Defender not involved in a double team must learn to read the player with the ball and anticipate where the pass may be thrown. See Appendix A–V, Passing and Receiving Passes; Appendix B–I, On-the-Ball Defense; Appendix B–II, Off-the-Ball Defense.

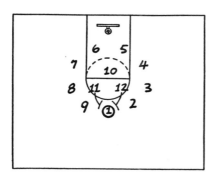

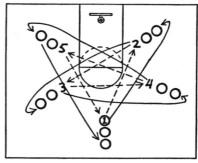

Diagram 11.4   Diagram 11.5

FIVE-CORNER DRILL

Purpose: For players to practice coming to meet a pass and work on chest and bounce passing.

Number of Personnel: A minimum of five players to a maximum of fifteen.

Equipment and Facilities: One basketball and a half court.

Procedure: Coach should make sure the players are coming to meet the ball. Player 1 passes to Player 2 and follows pass to the end of that line (see Diagram 11.5). Player 2 passes to 3 and follows. Player 3 passes to 4 and follows. Player 4 passes to 5 and follows. The process is then continued. A simple rule for the players to remember is that they can not pass to a line next to them nor to the line from which they received the pass. Since the players are coming to meet the pass, they will slowly close the gap between themselves from about fifteen to twenty feet to about five feet.

Time: Approximately 5 minutes.

Coaching Points: Coach must encourage players to perform drill with maximum effort. See Appendix A–V, Passing and Receiving Passes.

MACHINE-GUN DRILL

Purpose: Players learn to react quickly on passes and to "look" the basketball into their hands.

Number of Personnel: Groups of five or six players.

Equipment and Facilities: Two basketballs per group of players and a half court.

Procedure: One player should be about ten feet away from the other players facing him or her (see Diagram 11.6). One basketball is in Player 1's hands and the other ball is held by any of the other players. Player 1 may pass to any of the facing players. As 1 passes, the player with the other ball passes to 1. Player must throw the ball up and down the line as quickly as possible.

Time: Each player out in front should do the drill for 30 seconds to 1 minute.

Coaching Points: Emphasis should be placed on quickness of release, accuracy of the pass, and "looking" the ball into the hands each time. See Appendix A–V, Passing and Receiving Passes.

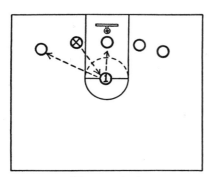

Diagram 11.6

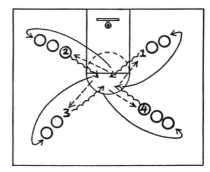

Diagram 11.7

DRIBBLE, PIVOT, PASS DRILL

Purpose: Players work on dribbling, pivoting, and passing techniques.

Number of Personnel: A minimum of four to a maximum of twenty players.

Equipment and Facilities: Two basketballs and a half court.

Procedure: Coach should divide team into four squads. Players stand approximately twenty-five feet apart (see Diagram 11.7). A ball is given to Players 2 and 4, who dribble with their left hand to the middle, plant their right foot and pivot, facing the squad to their right. 1 and 3 receive the passes. Players follow their pass to the end of that line. The process is then repeated. The coach could also have them pivot left.

Time: 5 to 10 minutes.

Coaching Points: When making the pivot, players should swing their leg opposite the pivot foot back in the direction of their line in order to face the squad to their right. See Appendix A–V, Passing and Receiving Passes; Appendix A–I, Ball Handling.

HALF-COURT BASEBALL-PASS DRILL

Purpose: Players practice proper leading techniques for a baseball pass.

Number of Personnel: A minimum of four players to a maximum of sixteen.

Equipment and Facilities: Two basketballs and a half court.

Procedure: The drill begins with Player 1 dribbling toward the other sideline (see Diagram 11.8). Player 2 runs towards the same sideline and then cuts to basket. Player 1 hits 2 with a baseball pass at approximately the free throw line. Player 1 goes behind 2's line, and 2 goes behind 1's line.

Time: 3 to 5 minutes depending on number of participating players.

Coaching Points: Coach must instruct players receiving the pass to look the ball into their hands. Make sure players are cutting hard to the basket. See Appendix A–V, Passing and Receiving Passes; Appendix A–II, Shooting.

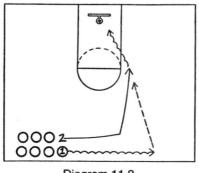
Diagram 11.8

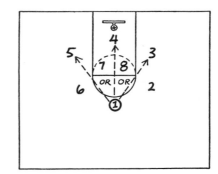
Diagram 11.9

TWO-BULLS-IN-THE-RING DRILL

Purpose: Offensive players learn pass to avoid defensive players, while defensive players improve their ability to anticipate a pass.

Number of Personnel: Groups of seven or eight players and a coach.

Equipment and Facilities: One or two basketballs per group, and up to two groups of players on a half court.

Procedure: Players 7 and 8 act as the bulls in the middle of the circle (see Diagram 11.9). The other players on the circle cannot pass to a person next to them. They must keep the ball moving and not throw a pass higher than shoulder level. If one of the bulls touches or interrupts the pass, the passer and the bull exchange places.

Time: 5 to 10 minutes.

Coaching Points: Make sure circle is not spread out so far as to make it impossible for the defenders to deflect a pass. Defensive players are learning to read the offensive person and anticipate where the pass is to be thrown. Offensive players should also work on faking the passes in one direction and then going opposite. See Appendix A–V, Passing and Receiving Passes; Appendix B–II, Off-the-Ball Defense.

FOUR-CORNER PASSING DRILL

Purpose: Players practice making accurate passes of distance.

Number of Personnel: Minimum of eight players to a maximum of sixteen.

Equipment and Facilities: One or two basketballs and a half court.

Procedure: Coach should put a line of players in each corner of a half court (see Diagram 11.10). The ball is passed diagonally and then to the right each time. After a player makes a pass, he or she runs to where it was thrown. After a given period of time the coach may want to add a second basketball to the drill.

Time: 3 to 10 minutes.

Coaching Points: See Appendix A–V, Passing and Receiving Passes.

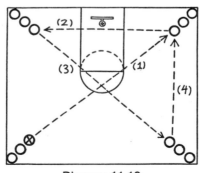

Diagram 11.10

TWO-LINE PASSING DRILL #1

Purpose: To practice making and meeting various types of passes.

Number of Personnel: Two to twenty players and a coach.

Equipment and Facilities: One basketball for each pair of players. If the coach has a limited number of basketballs, players can be placed in groups of three or four. A half court area will be sufficient space.

Procedure: Players pair up (see Diagram 11.11). Each pair has a basketball. Players pass back and forth to one another and should come to meet each pass. They can work on chest pass, bounce pass, curl pass, baseball pass, and so on.

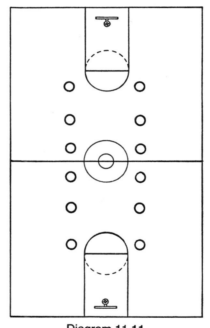

Diagram 11.11

Time: 3 to 5 minutes.

Coaching Points: Coach should emphasize need for accuracy in the pass and encourage players to give maximum effort at all times during the drill. See Appendix A–V, Passing and Receiving Passes.

TWO-LINE PASSING DRILL #2

Purpose: To work on making and meeting various types of passes.

Number of Personnel: Two to twenty players.

Equipment and Facilities: A basketball per pair of players, either a half court or a full-court, depending upon the number of participating players, and a whistle.

Procedure: One line has the basketballs. At the first whistle, the other line runs away. At the second whistle they come back to the ball as players with the basketballs throw either chest, overhead, or baseball passes.

Time: 3 to 5 minutes.

Coaching Points: Emphasis is on fundamentals. See Appendix A–V, Passing and Receiving Passes.

TWO-LINE PASSING DRILL #3

Purpose: Players practice ball handling and quick-touch passes.

Number of Personnel: A minimum of ten players to a maximum of twenty and a coach.

Equipment and Facilities: One basketball and a half court.

Procedure: Ball starts at one end and every player must touch it all the way to the other end. The coach sets a time limit for players to complete the drill, depending on number involved in the drill.

Time: Coach determines duration.

Coaching Points: Stress the quickness of touch passes in drill because of the time limit involved. See Appendix A–V, Passing and Receiving Passes.

TWO-LINE PASSING DRILL #4

Purpose: Players practice quick reactions on passes in a competitive situation.

Number of Personnel: An even number of players between twelve and twenty, and a coach.

Equipment and Facilities: Two basketballs and a half court.

Procedure: Coach divides players into two groups with two lines facing each other in each group. Players will be competing on quickness of passing. Coach can vary the type of pass the players must use and have each player touch the ball once, twice, three times and so on. The coach should make the competition a best of five.

Time: Depends on how quickly the competition is completed.

Coaching Points: A fun drill for players because of the competition. Quickness of the catch and release is the key. See Appendix A–V, Passing and Receiving Passes.

THREE-PLAYER
FULL-COURT PASSING DRILL

Purpose: Players learn to make passes while on the move.

Number of Personnel: Six to eighteen players and a coach.

Equipment and Facilities: Two basketballs and a full court.

Procedure: Three players fill the lanes and pass the ball back and forth while going up and back down the court (see Diagram 11.12). The ball is not to touch the floor. No shots are taken. Players can first do the drill with one ball and later add a second ball.

Time: Coach determines duration.

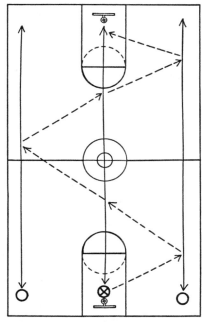

Diagram 11.12

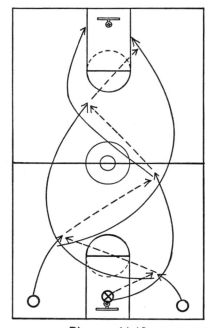

Diagram 11.13

Coaching Points: Drill is to be done at full speed. Stress accuracy of passes and looking the ball into the hands each time. See Appendix A–V, Passing and Receiving Passes.

THREE-PLAYER-WEAVE, FULL-COURT DRILL

Purpose: To teach players to pass while on the move and make a driving lay-up.

Number of Personnel: Six to eighteen players and a coach.

Equipment and Facilities: At least two basketballs and a full court.

Procedure: Ball starts in the middle (see Diagram 11.13). Middle player passes to one of the sides and runs behind. Person receiving pass then passes to the third player and runs behind. Players continue the process all the way up the court and back. The coach can add a lay-up at one or both ends of the court.

Time: Duration determined by coach.

Coaching Points: Players must give maximum effort. Coach must encourage players to throw accurate passes and look the ball into their hands each time. See Appendix A–V, Passing and Receiving Passes; Appendix A–II, Shooting.

TWO-PLAYER SHUFFLE-AND-PASS, FULL-COURT DRILL

Purpose: Players pass while on the move and work on their shuffling techniques.

Number of Personnel: Eight to twenty players and a coach.

Equipment and Facilities: At least two basketballs and a full court.

Procedure: Four players can do the drill at one time. Two players face each other and never cross their feet while passing a ball between them up to one end line and back down the court (see Diagram 11.14). Players begin with chest passes and wait for coach to signal for a bounce pass. No shots are taken. The coach could have players run full speed and pass back and forth, or make each repetition a competitive drill.

Time: Coach determines duration.

Coaching Points: Coach should often remind players to work hard. Excellent drill for the early season because it will help with conditioning. Players

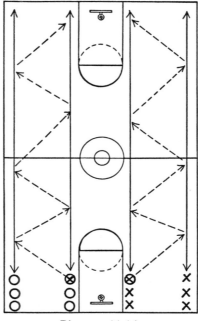

Diagram 11.14

must stay low when shuffling in order to go at maximum speed. See Appendix A–V, Passing and Receiving Passes.

PASSING DRILL WITH TIME LIMIT

Purpose: Players practice passing to avoid a defensive player.

Number of Personnel: Three players per group.

Equipment and Facilities: One basketball per group, and enough space to accommodate participating players.

Procedure: Players work in groups of three, with two offensive players standing approximately lane-width apart and a defensive player moving between them to attack the player with the ball (see Diagram 11.15). Offensive players must pass the ball within three seconds. Defensive player counts one-thousand one, one-thousand two, one-thousand three. Offensive players may not make a pass above the shoulder. The defensive player will stay in that role until: (a) player deflects a ball, (b) an offensive player violates one of the rules, or (c) the defensive player has been in the role for 30 seconds. The coach should then rotate the responsibilities of the players.

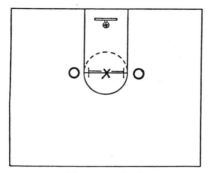

Diagram 11.15

Time: 3 to 5 minutes.

Coaching Points: Defensive player must be encouraged to give maximum effort and move toward ball on each pass. See Appendix A–V, Passing and Receiving Passes.

POOR PASS DRILL

Purpose: Players work on handling bad passes.

Number of Personnel: Two to sixteen players and coach.

Equipment and Facilities: A basketball for each pair of players and enough space to accommodate participating players.

Procedure: Players work in pairs from the various offensive positions on the floor. They should work in guard-guard, guard-forward, guard-center, forward-forward, and forward-center combinations. Players should make bad passes which are still catchable to one another so that they get in the habit of catching poor passes and then getting in proper position within the offense. Coach should emphasize with the players that their bad passes are intentional and hit a target.

Time: 2 to 5 minutes.

Coaching Points: Coach may want to dictate the type of pass to be thrown. See Appendix A–V, Passing and Receiving Passes.

THREE-ON-THREE DRILL

Purpose: To teach players to use passing to advance against pressure and to move without the basketball. Helps with defense and conditioning.

Number of Personnel: A minimum of six players to a maximum of twelve and a coach.

Equipment and Facilities: One basketball and a half court, or a full court for more than twelve players.

Procedure: The drill uses three offensive and three defensive players (see Diagram 11.16). Offensive players are allowed to take only one dribble and are not to make any long or lob passes. They must work the ball from out of bounds to up past half court. Defensive players play tough deny defense. When the offense gets past half-court, the two groups switch assignments (offense to defense and vice versa). Now the new offensive team works from half-court and tries to get ball past the original endline.

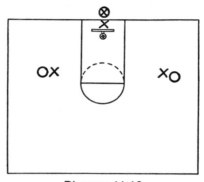

Diagram 11.16

Time: Coach determines duration.

Coaching Points: Coach should emphasize to players the need to move without the basketball in order to receive a pass. See Appendix A–V, Passing and Receiving Passes; Appendix A–IX, Movement Without the Ball; Appendix B–I, On-the-Ball Defense; Appendix B–II, Off-the-Ball Defense.

FULL-COURT PASSING DRILL

Purpose: To practice handling the basketball, make accurate passes, and execute lay-ups on the move.

Number of Personnel: Minimum of six players to a maximum of twelve and a coach.

Equipment and Facilities: One basketball for the first six players, an additional one for each player above six, and a full court.

Procedure: The coach should set up players as shown in Diagram 11.17, with four players in the key areas and one at each end line. Players start by

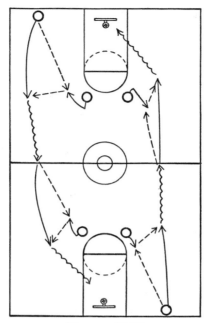

Diagram 11.17

working to the right side of the court. The four players receiving passes must run to meet the pass. The two shooting players must go as quickly as possible, mixing in dribbling and passing, and shoot a lay-up. The coach should run the drill for 30 seconds to 1 minute and then rotate the players.

Time: Time will depend upon the number of participating players.

Coaching Points: Could make drill competitive by having two full courts competing against one another or demanding a given number of successful lay-ups in a determined time period. This will ensure that players are performing the drill at maximum speed. See Appendix A–V, Passing and Receiving Passes; Appendix A–II, Shooting; Appendix A–I, Ball Handling.

STAR PASSING DRILL

Purpose: Players work on various types of passes.

Number of Personnel: Minimum of five players to a maximum of twenty.

Equipment and Facilities: One basketball, a half court, and tape to mark the floor.

Procedure: The drill starts with players set up in the five lines as shown in Diagram 11.18. The coach may designate which type of pass is to be

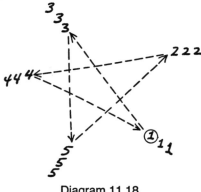

Diagram 11.18

worked on—chest, bounce, baseball, etc. Coach should also mark the five spots on the floor with tape to show the players where each line is to be positioned. Players must remember the following three rules: (1) they may not pass to a line next to them (2) they may not pass to a line from which they have just received a pass (3) players should always follow their pass and run to the end of the line to which they just passed. They must also make sure to stay out of the path of the next pass.

Time: Coach determines duration.

Coaching Points: Must make sure that players hustle from one line to the other. See Appendix A–V, Passing and Receiving Passes.

FOUR-CORNER PASSING
AND DRIBBLE DRILL

Purpose: To practice dribbling, passing, and pivoting skills.

Number of Personnel: Minimum of eight players to a maximum of sixteen.

Equipment and Facilities: Two or three basketballs and a half court.

Procedure: Two balls are used and started in opposite corners (see Diagram 11.19). At the whistle, players with basketballs dribble toward the line to their right. After two or three dribbles, they execute a two-hand chest pass and receive pass back immediately. They then dribble and hand ball off to the person from whom they just received the pass. The player who just handed off the ball goes to the end of that line. The new player with the basketball now executes the same procedure, moving toward the line to the right.

Time: Coach determines duration.

Coaching Points: When handing ball off, players must make proper pivot.

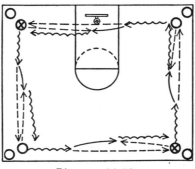

Diagram 11.19

They should plant the inside foot, swing other leg back towards the middle of the court, and put ball in inside hand in order to give it to the next person. At some point the coach may wish to use a third basketball in the drill. Players must give 100 percent at all times. Could also have players go to their left. See Appendix A–V, Passing and Receiving Passes; Appendix A–I, Ball Handling.

TWO-CIRCLE DRILL

Purpose: Players execute quick passes while moving in a circle.

Number of Personnel: Nine to ten players and a coach.

Equipment and Facilities: One basketball, a center jump circle or a similar-sized area, and a coach's whistle.

Procedure: Three players are on the inside and run in a circle in one direction (see Diagram 11.20). One of these three players has a basketball.

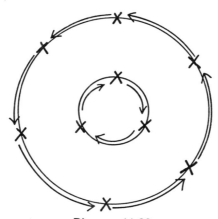

Diagram 11.20

Six players form a circle approximately six feet from the inner circle players and move in the opposite direction of the inner circle players. At the whistle, players move while passing the basketball back and forth from inner to outer circle and vice versa. Coach may designate the type of pass to be thrown—either a chest pass or a bounce pass. Every time the coach blows the whistle the players reverse the direction of their movement.

Time: Coach determines duration.

Coaching Points: Coach must make sure that proper distance is maintained between the inner and outer circles. Emphasis is on being aware and prepared to receive a pass. See Appendix A–V, Passing and Receiving Passes.

TOUCH DRILL

Purpose: For players to practice handling the basketball. Develops softness in catching and quickness in releasing the ball.

Number of Personnel: Entire team.

Equipment and Facilities: One basketball and a half court.

Procedure: Players line up in opposite corners of the half court. They then move continuously as indicated in Diagram 11.21. They are to touch pass the ball between them as they are moving and make sure that the ball does not touch the floor.

Time: 2 to 4 minutes.

Coaching Points: This drill can be used as a pre-game warm-up. Players go at approximately half-speed. See Appendix A–V, Passing and Receiving Passes

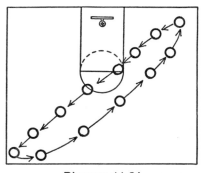

Diagram 11.21

SPOT PASSING DRILL

Purpose: For players to practice making accurate chest and bounce passes while performing on a time limit.

Number of Personnel: One player does the drill at a time. Someone should be present to keep time and record the number of successful passes.

Equipment and Facilities: One basketball, a wall, tape to mark spots on the wall, and a stopwatch.

Procedure: Tape is used to make two squares of approximately eighteen inches in width on a wall. The square to the left is about four feet up on the wall and the square to the right is three feet away from it and about two or three feet up on the wall. Players are to be placed ten to twelve feet from the wall and must make a chest pass into the left box and then a bounce pass into the right box. They continue alternating the chest pass and the bounce pass, and get one point for each time the ball is passed into a box. The drill can be used as a competiton among several players or as a way for players to challenge themselves to improve their passing accuracy.

Time: 30 to 60 seconds.

Coaching Points: See Appendix A–V, Passing and Receiving Passes.

OFFENSIVE MOVE DRILLS

JAB STEP AND CROSSOVER DRILLS

Purpose: To teach players the various possible moves off a jab step and how to get open to receive a pass.

Number of Personnel: A minimum of two players to a maximum of ten and a coach.

Equipment and Facilities: One or two basketballs and a half court.

Procedure: The offensive player starts on the wing and goes toward the box on that side of the lane (see Diagram 12.1). When player reaches the box he or she plants the right foot if on the right side of the court and the left foot if on the left side. Player pivots to go back up the lane toward the coach (or passer). When player comes up towards the ball, he or she gives outside hand as a target for the passer. While receiving the pass player makes sure to establish the proper pivot foot. If the player is right handed the left

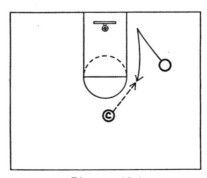

Diagram 12.1

foot is used as a pivot foot, and if left handed, uses the right foot. Player then squares up, faces the basket, and works on the following moves:

1. Throw jab step right at the defensive player. Extend step and drive to hoop for lay-up.
2. Throw jab step at the defensive player and shoot directly off the jab step.
3. Throw jab step at the defensive player and then take one hard dribble to the side, square up, and shoot jump shot.
4. Throw jab step at the defensive player, cross over with the jab foot, and drive to the hoop for a lay-up.
5. Throw jab step at the defensive player, cross over with the jab foot for one hard dribble, square up to basket, and shoot jump shot.

The coach can add defense to these drills and should also work on both sides of the floor.

Time: Coach determines duration.

Coaching Points: When adding defense to the drills, before having the offensive player react to the movement of the defender, coach may want defense to react to the jab step in a designated fashion so offensive player must perform a desired move. See Appendix A–VI, Outside Moves; Appendix B–I, On-the-Ball Defense.

RETURN SERIES

Purpose: To teach players the various options available off the pass-and-go behind maneuver.

Number of Personnel: A minimum of two players to a maximum of ten and a coach.

Equipment and Facilities: One or two basketballs and a half court.

Procedure: The drill uses two players, a guard and a forward. The forward takes guard to the basket just as in the Jab Step and Crossover Drill. The guard passes the ball to the forward and then goes behind to get the handoff (see Diagram 12.2). Guard now works on the following three plays:

1. Player gets handoff and drives directly to the basket for a lay-up.
2. Player gets handoff and hits jumper either immediately after handoff or by taking one dribble to the side.
3. Player gets handoff from the forward, dribbles toward baseline, and looks to hit forward on the roll to the basket.

The coach can add defense and run drill on both sides of the floor.

Time: Coach determines duration.

Coaching Points: Coach may elect to tell defense what to do when first adding them into the drill. This will ensure that the offense performs a desired move and learns to react to moves of the defense. See Appendix A–VIII, Setting and Using Screens; Appendix B–II, Off-the-Ball Defense.

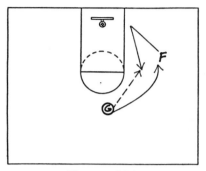

Diagram 12.2   Diagram 12.3

BONAVENTURE SERIES

Purpose: Players learn the proper technique to go away from the basketball and seal off defensive player on cut to the basket.

Number of Personnel: A minimum of two players to a maximum of ten and a coach.

Equipment and Facilities: One or two basketballs and a half court.

Procedure: The drill is run with two players, a guard and a forward (see Diagram 12.3). Forward moves as in the Jab Step and Crossover Drill to get open to receive a pass from the guard. Guard takes defensive player away and then seals him or her off and cuts to basket. In order to seal player off, the guard plants the foot nearest the basket, pivots on it, and swings other leg behind it and towards the basket.

Time: Coach determines duration.

Coaching Points: Offensive player cutting to the basket should set guard up for the give-and-go by first taking defender away from where the ball was passed. Cut to basket must be hard. Offensive player may also be able to cut immediately to basket without going away and sealing the defender, if the defensive player's position when the pass is thrown allows the offense to gain a step. Drill should be done first with no defense and later with it. See Appendix B–II, Off-the-Ball Defense.

SCREEN OPPOSITE DRILL

Purpose: Players practice the pass and screen away technique.

Number of Personnel: A minimum of three to a maximum of twelve players and a coach.

Equipment and Facilities: One or two basketballs and a half court.

Procedure: Run drill with three players, a guard and two wings. Forward moves as in the Jab Step and Crossover Drill in order to get open to receive a pass (see Diagram 12.4). Guard passes to the forward and then screens for the opposite wing. The wing cuts to the basket and guard pops back for a possible return pass and jumper. Forward may pass to either player.

Time: Coach determines duration.

Coaching Points: Offensive players should try to maintain their spacing. If player coming off screen looks for jump shot, then screener stays on that wing or looks to cut to basket. See Appendix A–VIII, Setting and Using Screens; Appendix B–II, Off-the-Ball Defense.

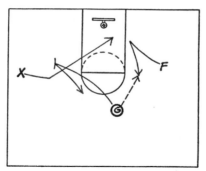

Diagram 12.4

REPLACE SERIES

Purpose: Players work on the guard, going away to set screen and then coming back to replace themselves.

Number of Personnel: A minimum of three players to a maximum of twelve and a coach.

Equipment and Facilities: One or two basketballs and a half court.

Procedure: The drill is run with three players, a guard and two wings. Forward moves as in the Jab Step and Crossover Drill in order to begin (see

Diagram 12.5). Guard passes to the forward, goes away from pass, and comes back to replace him or herself. Opposite wing fakes coming to the top of the key and then plants far foot from the basket and cuts to basket.

Time: Coach determines duration.

Coaching Points: This is a variation on the screen opposite drill. Offensive players fake the setting of a screen. See Appendix A–VIII, Setting and Using Screens; Appendix B–II, Off-the-Ball Defense.

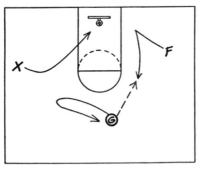

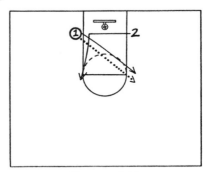

Diagram 12.5   Diagram 12.6

HAWK DRILL #1

Purpose: Players practice give-and-go move.

Number of Personnel: Two players at a time.

Equipment and Facilities: A basketball and a half court.

Procedure: Drill starts when Player 1 rolls ball towards opposite foul line extended and goes and gets it (see Diagram 12.6). Player 1 then pivots and squares to the basket. As soon as ball is rolled, 2 goes to the opposite box and then up to corner of foul line. Player 1 now passes to 2, fakes toward 2 and then cuts down lane. Player 2 makes a bounce pass to 1, follows for rebound, and takes ball to the box and rolls ball out. Players now repeat the process. Coach can designate the type of shot to be taken at end (lay-up, baby hook, etc.). Players should also switch to the opposite side of the floor.

Time: Two players run drill for 30 to 60 seconds.

Coaching Points: Coach must encourage players to give maximum effort throughout the duration of the drill. Cutter to basket on give-and-go move should give target to passer.

HAWK DRILL #2

Purpose: For defensive player to learn to block shots with the proper hand.

Number of Personnel: Two players at a time.

Equipment and Facilities: A basketball and a half court.

Procedure: Players move as in Hawk Drill #1 (see Diagram 12.6) except that player who picks up the rolled ball makes a one-dribble move to the basket for the shot and the other player moves to block shot with inside arm.

Time: Two players run drill for 30 to 60 seconds.

Coaching Points: Shooter must concentrate on lay-up and not worry about defender going for the block. See Appendix A–II, Shooting; Appendix B–I, On-the-Ball Defense.

HAWK DRILL #3

Purpose: To teach defensive players quickly to get position to cut off drive to the basket, while offensive players learn to avoid committing the charge and to move to the basket for the score.

Number of Personnel: Two players at a time.

Equipment and Facilities: One basketball and a half court.

Procedure: Players use the same start as in Hawk Drill #1 (see Diagram 12.6). Then the player who catches rolled ball squares and drives straight down line on lane. The other player goes to the opposite box, then halfway up the lane, and then over to cut off offensive player on the drive. Offensive player must execute either a crossover dribble or spin dribble to avoid being called for the charge.

Time: Two players run drill for 30 to 60 seconds.

Coaching Points: Players must be encouraged to give maximum effort throughout the drill. See Appendix A–I, Ball Handling; see Appendix A–II, Shooting; Appendix B–I, On-the-Ball Defense.

HAWK DRILL #4

Purpose: Offensive and defensive players work on a one-on-one situation.

Number of Personnel: Two players at a time.

Equipment and Facilities: A basketball and a half court.

Procedure: Players use same beginning as in Hawk Drill #1 (see Diagram 12.6) except defensive player goes to the opposite box and then on a diagonal to guard the offensive player. The offensive player squares to basket and then gets only one dribble to make a move to the basket, and may also take a jump shot.

Time: Two players run drill for 30 to 60 seconds.

Coaching Points: Encourage players to hustle at all times. Drill creates a one-on-one situation. Offensive player works on the jab step and shooting. See Appendix A–VI, Outside Moves; Appendix A–II, Shooting; Appendix B–I, On-the-Ball Defense.

PICK AND ROLL DRILL

Purpose: To teach players proper execution of the two player game.

Number of Personnel: A minimum of two players to a maximum of twelve and a coach.

Equipment and Facilities: One or two basketballs and a half court.

Procedure: Players work on the two-player game from various spots on the floor. Coach may elect not to use defensive players in the beginning in order to teach players how to set up and use a pick and how to set a pick and roll open. The coach can add defensive players later if he or she desires.

Time: 3 to 10 minutes.

Coaching Points: May begin drill one of two ways: (1) player passes to teammate on the perimeter and then goes to set a screen; or (2) player starts with the ball at a given spot on the perimeter, and teammate comes from some spot away from the ball to set the screen. Drill should be utilized primarily with a big man setting the screen for a perimeter player. See Appendix A–VIII, Setting and Using Screens; Appendix B–II, Off-the-Ball Defense.

MOVEMENT WITHOUT THE BALL DRILLS

Purpose: Players practice four moves without the basketball: the backdoor, button hook, square cut, dip, and the footwork necessary to execute each properly.

Number of Personnel: One to five players and a coach.

Equipment and Facilities: A half court.

Procedure: This is one of the most important aspects of the game and the least worked upon. The following four moves are essential in developing a complete player. In the following four drills, players begin on the right side

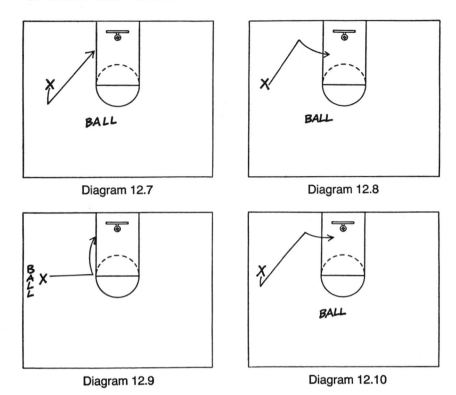

Diagram 12.7

Diagram 12.8

Diagram 12.9

Diagram 12.10

of court-foul line extended and execute each of the four moves. They should do each move three times on each side of the court.

1. *Backdoor:* Offensive player cuts behind defensive player to the basket, comes out towards the ball and plants the far foot from the basket, pushes off, and cuts towards basket. Player should not turn back to the ball. Players must give a target to the passer (see Diagram 12.7).

2. *Button Hook:* Offense takes defense to the basket, pivots on inside foot (foot closer to basket), opens up to the ball, pins defensive player on back and prepares to receive the pass (see Diagram 12.8).

3. *Square Cut:* Offense takes defense away from the ball to foul-line area, pivots on inside foot, opens up to the ball, pins defensive player on back, and prepares to receive the pass (see Diagram 12.9).

4. *Dip:* This is the move to make when a player is being overplayed. Player starts at the foul line extended and proceeds to execute a backdoor cut. When defensive player prevents by overplaying, offensive player simply takes a quick change of direction and "dips" in front of the defense toward the hoop (see Diagram 12.10).

Time: Time will depend on number of participating players.

Coaching Points: See Appendix A–IX, Movement Without the Ball.

SCREEN DRILL #1:
DOWN OR FRONT SCREEN

Purpose: Players learn to execute a down screen.

Number of Personnel: A minimum of three to a maximum of twelve players and a coach.

Equipment and Facilities: One or two basketballs and a half court.

Procedure: Coach should first do all of these drills using no defensive players and then add them to guard players setting screens. Later, coach may also add defensive players to guard player with ball. Make sure to work on both sides of the court.

Player closest to the foul line moves down to set screen for the player on the box (see Diagram 12.11). He or she should set a good, solid screen with a wide base on the defensive player. After player sets the screen, he or she should pivot on the foot closest to the basket and open up to the basketball while giving a target. The offensive player using the screen should set up his or her guard by taking him or her away from the screen and then run them into the screen. When player pops out, he or she is looking for the jump shot. Player should try to get behind the ball off the pass if possible. If player does not have jump shot, he or she should look to pass to post inside player. Players must learn to wait for the screens to be set.

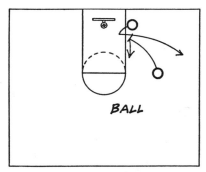

Diagram 12.11

Time: Coach determines duration.

Coaching Points: See Appendix A–VIII, Setting and Using Screens; Appendix B–II, Off-the-Ball Defense.

SCREEN DRILL #2:
UP OR BACK SCREEN

Purpose: To teach players proper method of making a back screen.

Number of Personnel: A minimum of three to a maximum of twelve players and a coach.

Equipment and Facilities: One or two basketballs and a half court.

Procedure: Player B, who is closest to the basket (see Diagram 12.12), moves up to screen for the perimeter player (Player A). Player A sets up the screen by moving in the opposite direction of the cut off the screen. Player B pops back, looking for pass after setting the screen. If the defensive players switch, then Player B keeps the defensive player he or she screens on their back and tries to get pass towards the basket which is away from the defensive player.

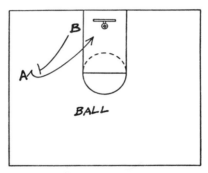

Diagram 12.12

Time: Coach determines duration.

Coaching Points: See Appendix A–VIII, Setting and Using Screens; Appendix B–II, Off-the-Ball Defense.

SCREEN DRILL #3:
LOW EXCHANGE

Purpose: Players practice proper execution of the low exchange.

Number of Personnel: A minimum of three to a maximum of twelve players and a coach.

Equipment and Facilities: One or two basketballs and a half court.

Procedure: The player on the ballside box (A) moves away to screen for the player on the opposite box (B) (see Diagram 12.13). Player B must wait for the screen and may go either to foul line side or to baseline side off the screen. Player A, who sets the screen, should seal back toward the ball moving toward the ballside high post.

Time: Coach determines duration.

Coaching Points: See Appendix A–VIII, Setting and Using Screens; Appendix B–II, Off-the-Ball Defense.

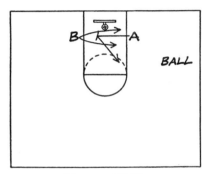

Diagram 12.13

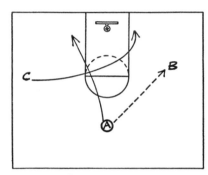

Diagram 12.14

SCREEN DRILL #4: SHUFFLE CUT

Purpose: To teach players proper execution of the shuffle cut.

Number of Personnel: A minimum of three to a maximum of twelve players and a coach.

Equipment and Facilities: One or two basketballs and a half court.

Procedure: Player A passes ball to player B and then cuts toward box on opposite side of foul lane (see Diagram 12.14). Player C executes a shuffle cut by cutting toward ball when pass is made to B. Player C should make contact with the rear of A as he or she makes cut. Rotation of players should be: A replaces C, C replaces B, and B goes to the end of the line where A began.

Time: Coach determines duration.

Coaching Points: Players should perform drill at maximum speed. Cuts must be executed immediately and at full speed. Defense can be added at a later date. See Appendix B–II, Off-the-Ball Defense.

THREE-PLAYER OFFENSIVE DRILL

Purpose: Offensive players work on the moves involved in a three-player game. They practice front or down screens, up or back screens, shuffle cuts, splits and posting up techniques. Defensive players learn to defend against those offensive moves.

Number of Personnel: A minimum of six players to a maximum of twelve and a coach.

Equipment and Facilities: One basketball and a half court.

Procedure: Drill pits three offensive players against three defensive players. Offensive players are positioned in the following three places on one side of a half court: one player on the box, another player on the wing toward the baseline and the third player above the foul line.

When the basketball is in the possession of the player above the foul line, there are four possible moves that can be made:

1. Front or down screen where the wing screens for the player on the box. The wing should post up after screening (see Diagram 12.15A).

2. The player on the box up- or back-screens for the player on the wing. After setting the screen, player pops back, looking for a quick jump shot. The wing cutting off the screen must look to post up if he or she does not get the pass for a lay-up (see Diagram 12.15B).

3. The ball is passed into the player on the box and a split is then run. The player above the foul line, who passed the ball to the box, sets a screen for the player on the wing. The offensive player on the box may pass to either player off the split (see Diagram 12.15C).

4. When the player on the box gets the basketball, he or she always has the option of making a good inside move for the score.

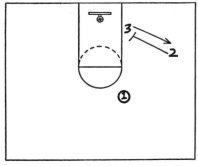

Diagram 12.15A

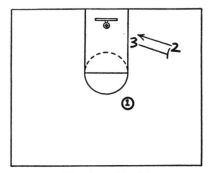

Diagram 12.15B

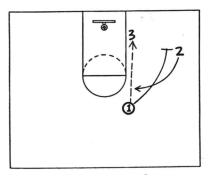

Diagram 12.15C

When the basketball is in the hands of the wing player, there are again four options available to the players:

1. The player above the foul line moves to set a down or front screen for the player on the box. The player on the box pops straight up the foul lane to look for a jump shot. The screener posts up after setting the screens (see Diagram 12.16A).

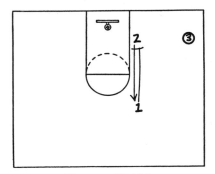

Diagram 12.16A

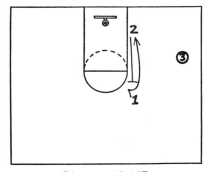

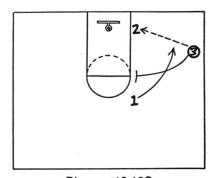

Diagram 12.16B   Diagram 12.16C

2. The offensive player on the box moves straight up the foul lane to set a pick for the player above the foul line. The player above the foul lane uses the screen and executes a shuffle cut to the basket. If that player does not get a pass for a lay-up, he or she posts up. The teammate setting the screen pops back afterwards to look for the jumper (see Diagram 12.16B).

3. The wing player can pass into the player on the box and then run a split. The passer always sets the screen. In this case the wing player sets a pick for teammate above the foul lane (see Diagram 12.16C).

4. If the player on the box receives a pass, then he or she can always execute a good inside move to try to score.

While executing the drill, the coach may wish his or her players to practice using only a few of the options listed above or may want them to freelance using all of the options mentioned.

Time: Duration will depend on the number of participating players. It is recommended that the drill last a minimum of 8 minutes to a maximum of 15.

Coaching Points: See Appendix A–VIII, Setting and Using Screens; Appendix B–II, Off-the-Ball Defense; Appendix B–I, On-the-Ball Defense.

REBOUNDING DRILLS

OUTLET DRILL

Purpose: Players learn proper rebounding and outletting techniques.

Number of Personnel: Minimum of three players to a maximum of twelve and a coach.

Equipment and Facilities: At least one basketball and a half court.

Procedure: Player R is the rebounder and throws the ball against the backboard and rebounds it (see Diagram 13.1). The coach must make sure R's arms are in an up position and that he or she does not bring the ball down after rebounding it. Rebounder should try to make half turn in air while grabbing rebound, and step toward the outlet player with the far foot from the basket. Then rebounder executes a two-handed overhead outlet pass to O, and becomes the new outlet player. O goes to the end of the line and a new rebounder steps forward. Players should work to both sides of the court.

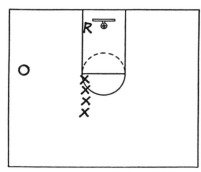

Diagram 13.1

To progress into this drill the coach may want players just to rebound the ball, keep it up, and not make an outlet pass. Coach could also have the rebounder box out the next player in line before going to get the rebound.

Time: 3 to 10 minutes.

Coaching Points: Coach should be checking for proper techniques. See Appendix B–III, Defensive Rebounding.

CIRCLE BOXING-OUT DRILL

Purpose: Defensive players work on proper blocking out maneuvers and maintaining contact with offensive players. Offensive player practices avoiding the box-out.

Number of Personnel: Minimum of two players to a maximum of eighteen players in pairs and a coach.

Equipment and Facilities: One basketball, a half court, and a whistle for the coach.

Procedure: Coach has a ball on the floor and arranges defensive players around it (see Diagram 13.2). A player can hold ball above head. An offensive player stands behind each defensive player. At the whistle, the offensive players try to get the ball while the defensive people box-out and try to keep them away from it. Defensive players should be able to do this for at least 3 seconds. Players work on proper boxing-out techniques and maintaining wide stance, good foot movement, and contact. Rotate players from defense to offense.

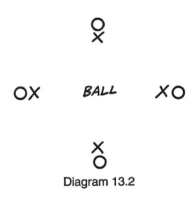

Diagram 13.2

Time: 3 to 5 minutes.

Coaching Points: Coach may want offensive players to go in a particular direction at the beginning of the drill. Coach should observe proper box-out techniques. At some point later in the season's practice, coach may also want to allow the offensive players to use one offensive rebounding technique to avoid the box-out. See Appendix B–III, Defensive Rebounding; Appendix A–VII, Offensive Rebounding.

BOXING-OUT DRILL

Purpose: To teach defensive players to box-out and then move aggressively to grab rebound. Offensive players try to avoid box-out and get offensive rebound.

Number of Personnel: Six to twelve players and a coach.

Equipment and Facilities: One basketball and a half court.

Procedure: Player C is the coach who shoots the ball to begin the drill. The drill can be done with two, four, or six players. Offensive players must start outside the lane (see Diagram 13.3). Defense should be in good defensive position and box-out their guarded players on the shot by the coach. Coach must make sure they box their players out and then move aggressively to basket for a good strong rebound. The coach can make the drill more competitive by telling defense to rebound three shots in three attempts or run, and can tell offense players they must rebound one shot in three attempts or run. Losers run a 10-second drill, then repeat the boxing out drill.

Time: Coach determines duration.

Coaching Points: Offensive players should be developing their offensive rebounding techniques. See Appendix B–III, Defensive Rebounding; Appendix A–VII, Offensive Rebounding.

SUPERMAN DRILL

Purpose: A good drill for conditioning and teaching players to rebound aggressively and on balance.

Number of Personnel: One player at a time.

Equipment and Facilities: One basketball, a basket, and possibly a stopwatch.

Procedure: Player starts drill by throwing ball off the backboard hard and catching it on other side of foul lane, landing on both feet and on balance (see Diagram 13.4). Player continues the process immediately for a period of time established by the coach. Later, after each catch outside lane, the coach could have the player make a designated inside move and then throw ball off backboard to other side of lane. Player must be constantly moving.

Time: Each player does drill twenty-five times or for 30 to 60 seconds.

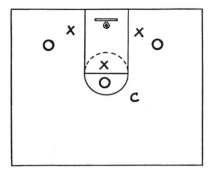 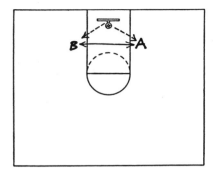

Diagram 13.3   Diagram 13.4

Coaching Points: To get player to perform the drill at maximum effort the coach can establish a set number of baskets that must be made in a given time period. See Appendix A–IV, Inside Moves.

TAPPING DRILL

Purpose: Players practice timing and quick jumping while keeping basketball on the backboard.

Number of Personnel: Two players at a time.

Equipment and Facilities: One or two basketballs and a basket.

Procedure: A player is positioned in each of Spots 1 and 2 (see Diagram 13.5). The object of the drill is for the players to tap the ball off the board back and forth to one another. A player can also do the drill on his or her own by keeping ball on one side of basket.

Time: Drill continues until players tap ball a set number of times (ten to twenty) or for 30 to 60 seconds.

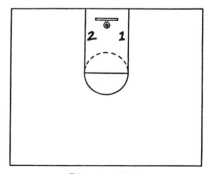

Diagram 13.5

Coaching Points: Players begin the drill again if they lose control of the basketball. See Appendix A–VII, Offensive Rebounding.

ANTE-OVER AND REBOUND DRILL

Purpose: Players work on footwork, timing, and jumping while keeping basketball on the backboard. Good conditioner.

Number of Personnel: Three players.

Equipment and Facilities: One basketball, a basket, and a stopwatch.

Procedure: Players should have hands up at shoulder level at all times during the drill. The drill starts when one player throws the ball up at the backboard so that it does not touch the rim. The ball starts on the side with two players. After each player rebounds and taps ball across the backboard, he or she moves to the other side of the basket (see Diagram 13.6). Players must keep the ball going.

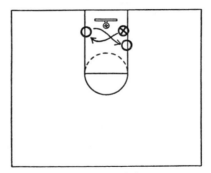

Diagram 13.6

Time: Players execute drill for 30 to 60 seconds.

Coaching Points: If players lose control of the ball, they begin again. Good early-season drill because it aids in conditioning. See Appendix A–VII, Offensive Rebounding.

TRAILER-AND-REBOUND DRILL

Purpose: Players practice speed dribble, rebounding, and outletting techniques. Also, a good conditioning drill.

Number of Personnel: Minimum of two players to a maximum of twenty and a coach.

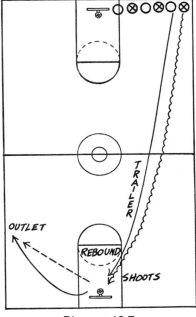

Diagram 13.7

Equipment and Facilities: A basketball for each pair of players and a full court.

Procedure: Players are lined up on one baseline in pairs. One player holds the ball and the other player acts as the trailer. The player with the ball speed dribbles the length of the court and shoots a lay-up (see Diagram 13.7). The trailer rebounds the ball using proper form and makes a strong outlet pass to the shooter, who continues to the outlet spot. Shooter drives length of floor and makes lay-up. The trailer again rebounds the shot. Players switch roles the next time through the drill.

Time: 5 to 10 minutes.

Coaching Points: Excellent drill to be used in the early season for conditioning. See Appendix A–I, Ball Handling; Appendix A–II, Shooting; Appendix B–III, Defensive Rebounding.

RELEASE DRILL

Purpose: Players practice proper rebounding and outletting techniques.

Number of Personnel: Two players.

Equipment and Facilities: One basketball and a half court.

Procedure: One player shoots the ball from the foul line. A second player stands in the middle of the lane and rebounds the shot. The shooter goes to the proper side of the floor for an outlet pass and the rebounder uses proper form to fit the side the rebound comes off. Rebounder makes a strong outlet pass.

Time: Drill runs for 1-minute time period, and then players switch assignments.

Coaching Points: Coach should stress proper techniques and encourage players to perform at maximum efficiency. See Appendix A–II, Shooting; Appendix B–III, Defensive Rebounding.

ANTICIPATION DRILL

Purpose: To improve players' timing in going after a rebound.

Number of Personnel: One to ten players and a coach.

Equipment and Facilities: One basketball, a basket, and a rebounder ring over the basket.

Procedure: Place a rebounder ring on the basket so that a shot cannot go in. The coach should have one player at about the midlane area. The coach throws the ball up toward the basket, and the player goes *aggressively* to get rebound. As time goes on, move player further away from the basket. Player is not allowed to let the ball hit the floor. Coach should also change angles of shots.

Time: Coach determines duration.

Coaching Points: It is important that the player learns to read the angle of the shot, distance, and effectiveness of shot in order to try to anticipate where the basketball will come off for the rebound. See Appendix B–III, Defensive Rebounding.

BURST-OUT DRILL

Purpose: To teach players to rebound aggressively using proper blocking-out and rebounding maneuvers and then breaking double-team pressure by dribbling.

Number of Personnel: A minimum of three players to a maximum of nine and a coach.

Equipment and Facilities: One basketball and a half court.

Procedure: The drill uses three players: one shooter, one defensive rebounder, and one offensive rebounder. Player 1 (see Diagram 13.8) shoots the basketball and X rebounds and fights through a double-team set by the shooter and offensive rebounder (O) by keeping body low. The coach can have the players rotate positions or set up a line behind the shooter and work a rotation out of that situation. If the defensive rebounder allows offense to get a rebound, then defensive player should be made to run.

Time: Coach determines duration.

Coaching Points: Defensive rebounder should use proper techniques in order to get the ball off the glass first and then try to split the intense double-team pressure. Defensive player must protect ball at all costs and cannot give the ball back to offense under their own basket. See Appendix B–III, Defensive Rebounding; Appendix A–VII, Offensive Rebounding; Appendix A–II, Shooting.

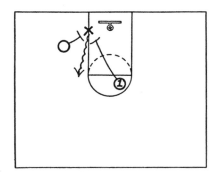 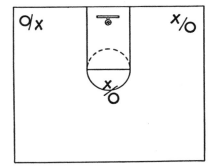

Diagram 13.8   Diagram 13.9

BASELINE BOX-OUT DRILL

Purpose: Defensive players practice boxing-out and going after rebound on missed shot, while offensive players work on offensive rebounding techniques.

Number of Personnel: A minimum of six to a maximum of twelve players and a coach or manager.

Equipment and Facilities: A half court and one basketball.

Procedure: The coach puts players in positions shown in Diagram 13.9. A coach or manager can shoot the ball. Players make initial box-out contact and then go aggressively to boards for the rebound. Coach can make it into a contest by telling defensive players they must rebound three shots in three attempts or run. Offensive players must rebound one shot in three attempts or run. Losers run a ten-second drill.

Time: Coach determines duration.

Coaching Points: Coach must observe closely both defensive and offensive rebounding techniques. See Appendix B–III, Defensive Rebounding; Appendix A–VII, Offensive Rebounding.

TEAM SCRAMBLE DRILL

Purpose: Defensive players work to keep offensive players from getting to the basketball.

Number of Personnel: Ten players and a coach.

Equipment and Facilities: A basketball and a half court.

Procedure: Coach places a ball on floor underneath the basket (see Diagram 13.10). Defensive players must make contact and keep the offensive players away from the ball for 3 to 5 seconds. This drill is the same as the circle box-out drill except five players are being used, and are put in a more spread position.

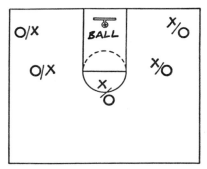

Diagram 13.10

Time: 3 to 5 minutes.

Coaching Points: Coach may not only wish to stress defensive box-out techniques but also the offensive players methods to avoid the block-out. Defensive people must move their feet in order to maintain contact. See Appendix B–III, Defensive Rebounding; Appendix A–VII, Offensive Rebounding.

TEAM BOX-OUT DRILL

Purpose: To teach players the footwork, form, and other techniques necessary to block a player out.

Number of Personnel: Any number of players and a coach.

Equipment and Facilities: Enough space to accommodate participating players.

Procedure: Players pair up and face coach. One of the pair will play offense and the other play defense. At the whistle, the offensive player will move in the direction specified by the coach. The defensive player uses proper technique for boxing-out the offensive player. The two players then switch roles.

Time: 2 to 5 minutes.

Coaching Points: This drill is very effective when first teaching defensive rebounding techniques. Can also be used just as effectively when beginning to teach offensive rebounding maneuvers. See Appendix B–III, Defensive Rebounding; Appendix A–VII, Offensive Rebounding.

TEAM FULL-COURT TAP DRILL

Purpose: A good conditioning drill. Players practice timing to keep basketballs on the backboards.

Number of Personnel: Any number of players and a coach or manager.

Equipment and Facilities: Two basketballs, a full court, and a stopwatch.

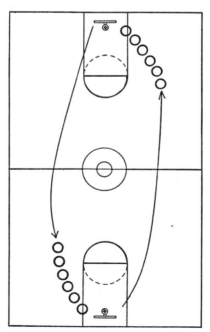

Diagram 13.11

Procedure: Coach lines players up on the same side of both baskets on a full court (see Diagram 13.11). The first player in each line throws the ball up on the board. Players continue tapping the balls and not letting them hit the floor. After tapping at one basket, player runs to end of line on the other basket.

Time: Players continue drill without letting ball hit the floor for anywhere from 60 seconds to 2 minutes.

Coaching Points: Drill is designed to be implemented primarily in the early season because of its conditioning value. See Appendix A–VII, Offensive Rebounding.

TWO-PLAYER BOX-OUT, SWITCH DRILL

Purpose: To make players move before executing boxing-out techniques.

Number of Personnel: A minimum of four players to a maximum of twelve and a coach or manager.

Equipment and Facilities: A half court and one or two basketballs.

Procedure: Two offensive players stand behind the foul line and outside the foul lane area (see Diagram 13.12). The two defensive players stand outside the foul lane and approximately six feet closer to the basket than the offensive players they are guarding. Coach (or manager) takes a shot. As soon as ball is released offensive players go to crash boards for an offensive rebound. Defensive players box-out opposite offensive players as shown in the diagram. Defensive players box-out and then crash for the rebound.

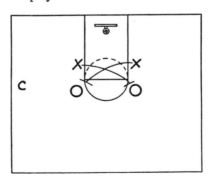

Diagram 13.12

Time: Coach determines duration.

Coaching Points: Drill is very challenging for players. They are learning to try to get position on an offensive player, quite a distance from them, who is crashing the boards. See Appendix B–III, Defensive Rebounding.

REBOUND DRILL

Purpose: Players practice rebounding and outletting techniques.

Number of Personnel: A minimum of four players to a maximum of twelve and a coach.

Equipment and Facilities: One basketball and a half court.

Procedure: Coach places a player at each wing position (2 and 3 in Diagram 13.13A) and a line out front at the top of the key (1, 4, and 5). The wings move to get a pass. The player at the point with the ball (1) passes to either wing and cuts to the basket. The wing returns pass and 1 throws the ball off the board and rebounds, making a strong outlet pass to either wing. Whichever wing receives pass sends ball back out to the next player in line (4) and goes to the end of the line. The rebounder (1) replaces the vacated wing and the process is repeated (see Diagram 13.13B).

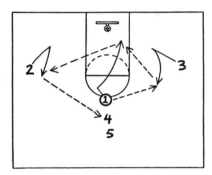
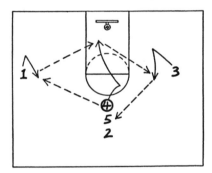

Diagram 13.13A   Diagram 13.13B

Time: 3 to 10 minutes.

Coaching Points: Cutter going to basket should go away from the wing who received the first pass and then make good, hard cut to the hoop. Coach can specify whether the wing should make a bounce or chest pass to the cutter. Players must hustle continuously. See Appendix B–III, Defensive Rebounding; Appendix A–V, Passing and Receiving Passes.

PRESSURE BOX-OUT DRILL

Purpose: Players learn to make a strong block-out.

Number of Personnel: Two players at a time and a coach.

Equipment and Facilities: A center-jump circle or the circle by the free-throw line.

Procedure: Drill begins with two players placed back to back in the middle of the foul line (see Diagram 13.14). They should stand straight upright. At the coach's whistle the players immediately assume good box-out position— wide base with feet, legs bent, arms and elbows up and locked, and making contact with their buttocks. Players exert pressure against each other by staying on the balls of their feet and try to force one another out of the circle. They must maintain a back-to-back position and not slide off to the side of the opponent. Drill can be made into a contest by making it best of five, seven, etc. Loser runs a 10-second drill.

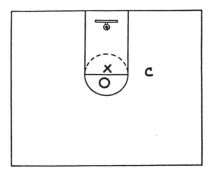

Diagram 13.14

Time: Time will depend on players.

Coaching Points: Coach should emphasize to players that the drill is designed to help players establish a strong, sturdy box-out position. The drill is not meant to suggest that, on a box-out, the defender is to move the opponent backwards ten feet or more. See Appendix B–III, Defensive Rebounding.

THREE-ON-THREE CONTEST DRILL

Purpose: Defensive players practice proper defensive positioning according to the position of the basketball and boxing-out and rebounding techniques. Offensive players work on avoiding block-out and going hard to the offensive glass.

Number of Personnel: A minimum of six players to a maximum of twelve, a coach, and a manager.

Equipment and Facilities: One basketball and a half court.

Procedure: This is primarily a drill for the front court players. It utilizes three offensive players and three defensive players. Forwards assume positions on each wing and the center should be in the low post area (see Diagram

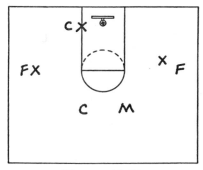

Diagram 13.15

13.15). A coach and a manager assume the two guard spots out front and pass the ball back and forth until one decides to shoot. Defensive players must make the proper defensive slides as the ball is passed out front. On the shot the players use proper offensive and defensive rebounding techniques. Three consecutive rebounds by either the offense or defense causes the losers to run a 30-second line drill.

Time: Coach determines duration.

Coaching Points: Players must learn to establish defensive rebounding position, even though they may be far from the offensive player they are guarding, due to defensive positioning. See Appendix B–III, Defensive Rebounding; Appendix A–VII, Offensive Rebounding; Appendix B–II, Off-the-Ball Defense.

FIVE-ON-FIVE
WITH REBOUNDER DRILL

Purpose: To work defense team on executing proper player-to-player defensive and rebounding techniques, while offensive team practices player-to-player offense and goes hard for offensive rebound.

Number of Personnel: Ten players at a time and coach or manager.

Equipment and Facilities: One basketball, a half court, and a rebounder ring.

Procedure: Drill starts with a rebounder ring over the rim so that no shot can go through basket. Offensive team runs a play designated by the coach. The defensive team plays good, solid player-to-player defense. Offense shoots at the first opportunity. Points are assigned in the following manner: one point for a defensive rebound, two points for an offensive rebound, two points for the defense if the offense commits a turnover, and one point for the defense if they force a jump ball situation. If the defensive team gets a rebound, they become the offensive team. If the offensive team gets a rebound, they continue to be the offensive team and bring the ball out to run the offense again. In a jump-ball situation, the defensive team becomes the offense. First team to score twenty-one points wins. Losers run a 30-second line drill.

Time: Duration depends on how long it takes one of the teams to reach twenty-one points.

Coaching Points: Coach must make sure that the offense executes the designated play and does not start to "cheat" to gain advantage for an offensive rebound. Coach must emphasize to offense that executing the play and not committing any turnovers are of primary importance. Defensive players must adhere to defensive player-to-player rules and not "cheat" for positioning on defensive rebounds. Coach may add or subtract points if he or she notices that the cheating is taking place. Drill utilizes a wide range of fundamentals.

SLIP, REBOUND, SPRINT, QUICK FEET DRILL

Purpose: Drill emphasizes various offensive rebounding maneuvers.

Number of Personnel: Six to eighteen players.

Equipment and Facilities: A full court.

Procedure: Begin drill by using three offensive and three defensive players. Defensive players box-out but try to let offensive players beat them. Three offensive players use one of the following offensive rebound techniques:

1. Step and go—where players step and fake in one direction and quickly move to basket in other direction.
2. Spin—they attack the defensive player's feet and spin around him or her using either foot as a pivot foot.
3. Hook step—players lock feet with the defensive rebounder in order to be on same standing as player is.

The two offensive wing players jump and touch the board as high as they can five times; the center also touches rim five times. All three players then sprint to free-throw area on opposite end of floor, turn, face defense, and do 10 seconds of quick feet (see Diagram 13.16). Rotation is as follows: three offensive players go off the floor, three defensive players become the offensive players, and three new players come on as the defensive players.

Time: Coach determines duration.

Coaching Points: Good early season drill because of conditioning for players and teaching offensive rebounding techniques. See Appendix A–VII, Offensive Rebounding.

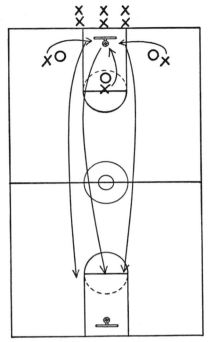

Diagram 13.16

REBOUND-AND-BREAK DRILL

Purpose: Team members work on both offensive and defensive rebounding skills with emphasis on positioning, boxing-out the opponent and outletting the basketball to begin a fast break. They also practice the team's fast break system and conversion from offense to defense.

Number of Personnel: Ten players and a coach or manager.

Equipment and Facilities: A full court and one basketball.

Procedure: The ten players are placed on two teams; one will be the offensive team and the other the defensive team. Offensive players start outside the foul lane and the defense work player-to-player (see Diagram 13.17). Coach begins drill by taking a shot from various spots on the floor. On the shot the defensive players leave their player and go aggressively to rebound the ball. The offensive team assumes offensive rebounding positions. Upon gaining control of the basketball, defense immediately looks to run a fast break for a quick score. At the same time the offensive team is converting quickly to defense to prevent the score. If the team running the fast break does not get a quick basket, then they run the team's secondary fast break while the other team plays player-to-player defense.

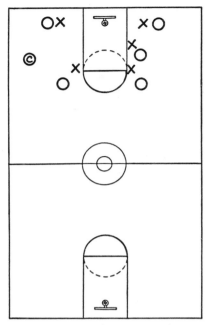

Diagram 13.17

The team that rebounds and runs the break continues in that role until one of two situations occurs: either they do not score on their fast break attempt, or the other team comes up with an offensive rebound off the original missed shot by the coach. After each fast break, whether the team scores or not, the ball is given back to the coach who resets the players and shoots to begin the drill once again.

Time: A minimum of 7 minutes to a maximum of 15.

Coaching Points: Coach will have to teach players where they should be for their offensive rebounding positions (one player back, one-and-a-half players back, etc.). See Appendix B–III, Defensive Rebounding; Appendix A–VII, Offensive Rebounding; Appendix C–III, Five-Player Fast-Break Rules.

COMPETITIVE
DRILLS

ANIMAL DRILL

Purpose: To teach players to go after a rebound aggressively and shoot strong inside shots with a player closely covering them.

Number of Personnel: A minimum of five players to a maximum of twelve and a coach.

Equipment and Facilities: One basketball and a basket.

Procedure: This drill can also be done as a rebounding and/or inside power move drill. Players usually enjoy this drill but it can be very tiring. There are three players on the court at a time, with other players underneath the basket and ready to jump in. The only way a player gets off the court is to score. The other two players try to stop the person with the ball from scoring. Players must score within the lane. There are no fouls. If the ball goes outside lane, it must be thrown back to the coach who is stationed about five feet below the foul line. No dribbles are needed. When a player scores, he or she goes off the floor and a new player takes part in the drill.

Time: 5 to 10 minutes.

Coaching Points: The coach must maintain strict supervision to be sure that the physical contact does not go to an extreme. The coach should also remind players that the drill is designed to increase aggressiveness in rebounding and to be strong when powering the ball up to the basket. Fouling is not to be carried over into normal competition. The coach should stop the drill immediately if the players begin to get carried away with the physical contact.

LOOSE-BALL DRILLS (Sets A–C)

Purpose: For coach to end practice in a competitive spirit with players hustling and practicing various basketball skills.

Number of Personnel: Entire team, split several squads depending upon number of available courts, and a coach.

Equipment and Facilities: Four basketballs per full court. The more full courts that can be used, the more effective the competition will be. Coach needs a whistle.

Procedure:

SET A (Diagram 14.1 shows positions of the basketballs.)

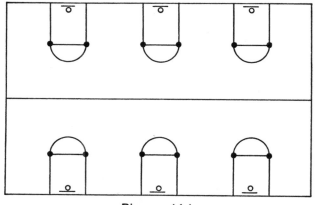

Diagram 14.1

Drill #1: Each team is stationed under a basket. Two players from each team begin drill at whistle by the coach. Each player gets a basketball at nearest foul line and then drives to make a lay-up. Lay-ups must be successful. After making lay-up, players grab ball and sprint to half-court. First team to have both players cross the midcourt line wins.

Drill #2: Each team is stationed under a basket. Two players from each team begin the drill at whistle by the coach. Each player goes to get a basketball at furthest foul line and then drives to make lay-up at nearest basket. Lay-ups must be successful. After making lay-up, players grab ball and sprint to half-court. First team to have both players cross the midcourt line wins.

Drill #3: Each team is stationed under a basket. Two players from each team begin the drill at whistle by the coach. Each player goes to get a basketball at the nearest foul line and then drives to make lay-up. Lay-ups must be successful. After making lay-up, one player grabs both basketballs and sprints to half-court. First team to have a player cross the midcourt line wins.

Drill #4: Each team is stationed under a basket. Two players from each team start the drill at whistle by the coach. One player goes to get one basketball and shoot a lay-up, then gets the other ball and shoot a lay-up. Lay-ups must be successful. Second teammate sprints to half-court and awaits the passes from his or her partner. First team whose player at half-court is holding both basketballs wins.

SET B (Diagram 14.2 shows positions of the basketballs.)

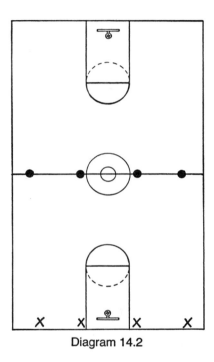

Diagram 14.2

Drill #1: Each team is positioned under a basket. Four players from each team go after each of the basketballs when the coach blows the whistle to start the drill. Two players go to each basket by using a speed dribble and make a lay-up. Lay-ups must be successful. All four players grab basketballs after the shot and run to half-court. First team to have all four players cross the midcourt line wins.

Drill #2: Each team is positioned under a basket. Four players from each team go after each of the basketballs when the coach blows the whistle to begin the drill. Two players go to each basket by speed dribbling and make a lay-up. Lay-ups must be successful. One player at each end of the court grabs both basketballs and runs to half-court. First team to have the two players cross the midcourt line wins.

SET C (Diagram 14.3 shows the positions of the basketballs.)

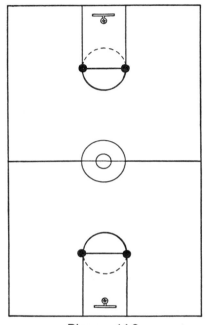

Diagram 14.3

Drill #1: Each team is stationed under a basket. Four players from each team sprint to half-court when the coach blows the whistle to start the drill. Two players go to each basket, pick up a basketball, and shoot a lay-up. Lay-up must be successful. Each player grabs a basketball and sprints back to half-court. First team to have all four players cross the midcourt line wins.

Drill #2: Procedure is the same as in Drill #1 except that one player at each basket grabs both basketballs and sprints to half-court. First team to get both players across the midcourt line wins.

Drill #3: Each team is positioned under a basket. Four players from a team sprint to half-court. Two of the players stay at half-court, and each of the other two go to a basket, pick up a ball and make a lay-up. They rebound shot and pass to a teammate at half-court. They then go to get second ball and make a lay-up, grab ball and pass it out to the same teammate at half-court. Both lay-ups must be successful. The first team to have the two players at midcourt holding two basketballs apiece wins.

Time: The drill continues until a team has won a total of five times. The team that accomplishes the task gets to leave practice. Other teams run a designated number of 10-second drills determined by the coach.

Coaching Points: Coaches must position themselves properly so as to be able to correctly determine the winner in each drill. Example: if the basketballs are being passed to the players stationed at half-court, the coaches should be stationed at either end of the mid-court line for proper vantage point for judging. The drills are designed to be used at the end of practice. A very good way to end practice on a high note.

HALF-COURT GAME

Purpose: For coach to work on a desired offense and defense in a competitive situation.

Number of Personnel: Ten players (five-on-five) and a coach.

Equipment and Facilities: A half court and one basketball.

Procedure: This drill allows a coach to work on both a desired offense and a desired defense. The defensive team becomes the offensive team if offense commits a total of three turnovers and/or is forced into jump ball situation, or if the offense does not score on four straight possessions.

Time: Coach determines duration.

Coaching Points: The coach must be aware of the results of each possession. The drill can be used with any offense and defense (zone or player-to-player). It is extremely effective in improving both offensive execution and defensive intensity. Can be done at any time during the season.

ZONE GAME

Purpose: Coach practices a desired zone offense and defense in a competitive situation.

Number of Personnel: Ten players (five-on-five), a coach, and a score-keeping manager.

Equipment and Facilities: One basketball and a half court.

Procedure: This drill allows coach to work on zone offenses. Play game to between twenty-one and thirty points. Losers run either a 30-second line drill, a seventeen-touch drill, or some other form of punishment desired by the coach. Winner could possibly be rewarded. Points are scored:

FOR OFFENSE

2 points for a basket

1 point for a foul on the defense or 2 points for foul in act of shooting

1 point for changing sides five or more times in zone offensive attack (if it applies)

1 point for an offensive rebound

FOR DEFENSE

3 points if they force the offense into a turnover

2 points for a defensive rebound

1 point if the offensive team does not execute the offense properly

2 points if they force a jump ball situation

Time: Will depend on how long it takes one team to reach the desired number of points.

Coaching Points: Coach must thoroughly know the point system for scoring. Every time points are scored the coach should call out the points awarded so as to make the job easier for the manager keeping score. This drill can be done at any time during the season. Excellent drill to increase intensity in the middle to end of the season.

PRESS OFFENSE
AND PRESS DEFENSE GAME

Purpose: Players work on foul shooting, press defense, and half-court defense, while offense practices press break offense and half-court offense in a competitive setting.

Number of Personnel: Ten players (five-on-five), a coach supervising, and a manager to keep score.

Equipment and Facilities: A basketball and a full court.

Procedure: Coach divides team into two squads, which, for the sake of explanation, will be designated as the red squad and the blue squad. The red team will determine a press defense in a huddle, and to begin the drill, the first player on the red team shoots a foul shot. The blue team must run an appropriate press offense and try to score at the other end. As soon as either a basket is made or the red team gets possession, the second player on the red team shoots a foul shot with a press defense being called in a huddle prior to the foul shot. Some procedure takes place. The blue team next sends their first shooter, then their second. The red team then shoots Players 3 and 4, and so on. Drill continues until a total of ten foul shots have been taken. The winning team is the one with the most points (including foul shots and baskets). Losing team runs either a 60-second line drill or a seventeen-touch drill.

Time: Duration will depend on how long it takes players to shoot the ten total foul shots.

Coaching Points: Coach should call out awarding of points so that manager and players are aware of the scoring. Fouls by the defense that cause either loss of possession or a missed field goal should count as two points being awarded to the offense. Drill can be run throughout the season.

PLAYER-TO-PLAYER
DEFENSE GAME

Purpose: To emphasize sound team player-to-player defensive principles by increasing intensity and concentration in a competitive situation. Offensive players work on player-to-player offense.

Number of Personnel: Ten players (five-on-five), a coach, and perhaps a manager.

Facilities and Equipment: A half court and one basketball.

Procedure: The ten players are divided into two teams. One squad practices player-to-player offense while the other team works on player-to-player defense principles. Points are assigned as follows for the defense: one point for each defensive rebound and one point for each time the offense commits a turnover. The offense earns points in the following ways: two points for each field goal, one point for each offensive rebound, one point for each non-shooting foul committed by the defense and two points for each shooting foul against the defense.

Time: The drill continues for either a 7- to 12-minute time period or until one team scores a total of twenty-five points.

Coaching Points: The coach must become very familiar with the point system and state when points are awarded so that the players and the person keeping score know. Drill can be used throughout the season. Especially valuable if there is a need to increase defensive intensity.

ZONE OFFENSE AND DEFENSE GAME

Purpose: For players to execute a given zone offense and zone defense designated by the coach. Competition increases concentration and intensity of the offense and the defense.

Number of Personnel: Ten players (five-on-five), a coach to instruct the defense and another coach for the offense, and perhaps a manager.

Equipment and Facilities: A half court and one basketball.

Procedure: The ten players are divided into two squads; one will execute a zone offense, and the other, a zone defense. If the coach wishes to emphasize defense then points should be assigned as follows: the offense gets two points for each time they score or are fouled in the act of shooting and the defense receives one point each time the offense does not score on a possession. If the coach is encouraging offensive execution then points are earned in this way: the offense gets one point each time they make a field goal or are fouled in the act of shooting and the defense receives two points each time the offense does not score on a possession.

Time: Drill lasts 7 to 12 minutes or until one team scores a total of twenty-one points.

Coaching Points: Can be performed any time during the season. Coach can stress offense or defense, dependent upon which is in the most need of improvement.

STATION DRILLS

WIDENER STATIONS

Purpose: Players practice various basketball and physical skills while getting excellent conditioning.

Number of Personnel: Up to twenty-four players, and two or three coaches.

Equipment and Facilities: A set of stairs, two jump ropes, eleven basketballs, three baskets, a whistle for one of the coaches keeping time, a stopwatch, and as much space as possible to accommodate the stations without crowding.

Procedure: Players go through stations in pairs. Each station runs for a full 60 seconds. At the 30-second mark the coach will blow a whistle for those stations at which it is necessary. Coach blows whistle twice for a change in stations. Players must sprint to the next station.

Station #1: Jump a line for 60 seconds (see Agility Section).

Station #2: Jump and turn 180° in air. Change direction of turn at 30-second mark.

Station #3: Run up and down steps for 60 seconds.

Station #4: Stationary ballhandling drills for 60 seconds (see Ball Handling section in Appendix).

Station #5: Jump rope for 60 seconds.

Station #6: Dribble for 60 seconds. Work on all the basic dribbles—speed, control, spin, crossover, stop and go, behind the back, and hockey step.

Station #7: Tap drill. Switch sides at 30-second mark. A player on each side of basket taps one of two balls against the backboard.

Station #8: Shuffle for 60 seconds. Players go back and forth in a given area.

Station #9: Ball reaction drill. Players switch assignments at 30-second mark. One player has ball and the other player stands with back to teammate. Player must keep looking straight ahead. Player with ball drops ball at various areas by player. Player must react quickly to grab ball.

Station #10: Pass reaction drill. Players switch assignments at 30-second mark (see Pass- and Turn-Around Drill, Chapter 1).

Station #11: Power-move drill. Players switch assignments at 30-second mark (see Power-Move Drill, Chapter 9).

Station #12: Jump-shot drill. Two players switch assignments at 30-second mark (see Two-Player Shooting Drill, Chapter 6).

Time: 12 minutes.

Coaching Points: These drills are ideal for early season practice. Players perform a variety of skill and conditioning drills. Coach must keep accurate track of time and move players from one station to the next quickly. He or she must also have the stations prepared (equipment at proper spots on floor) before practice begins. These drills should be done at the beginning of practice.

WESTHEAD CONTEST

Purpose: Emphasize shooting, lay-up, dribbling, and foot movement skills.

Number of Personnel: Up to forty-eight players per full court, a time-keeper, and four scorekeepers (one with each group).

Equipment and Facilities: Two baskets, a minimum of four basketballs, seven pylons, tape to mark the floor, a tossback or a wall, a stopwatch and a whistle for person keeping the time.

Procedure:

Station #1: Lay-ups (see Diagram 15.1). Players make as many lay-ups as possible in 30 seconds; one point for each successful lay-up. They must shoot lay-ups alternating sides on each shot.

Station #2: Players take 15' jump shots, making as many as they can in 30 seconds. Three points for each successful jumper. They must go back past the foul line for each jumper.

Station #3: Dribble through pylons. Players try to go past as many pylons as possible in 30 seconds. One point for each pylon passed. Count the starting pylon as one. One full trip through is eleven points.

Station #4: Wall bounce. Could use a toss-back. Put tape on the floor about four feet apart and three to four feet from wall. Players must get one

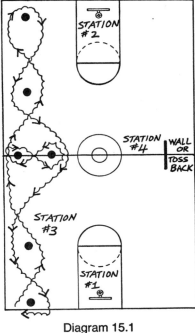

Diagram 15.1

foot outside the tape as they shuffle and bounce ball against a wall. One point for each time a foot gets outside the tape.

Each station runs for 30 seconds. The coach puts players in groups with an equal number of players at each of the stations. Scorekeeper stays with group for all four stations. Add up totals for each player at all four stations. Player with highest total wins the contest.

Time: If forty-eight players were to perform the contest, the total time it would take to complete the contest would be 24 minutes (thirty-two players—16 min; twenty-four players—12 min; twelve players—6 min).

Coaching Points: Should be used in the early season. Could be one method used to help determine abilities of players when cutting down a squad. Contest should be performed in the beginning of a practice. When the contest is completed, the winners (top one, two, or three) should be rewarded in some fashion by the coach.

ONE-COURT STATION DRILL #1

Purpose: Players work on the following skills: passing, handling a basketball off a pass, dribbling, foul shooting, and lay-ups.

Number of Personnel: Two to six players per station, timekeepers, and coaches.

Equipment and Facilities: Three basketballs plus one basketball for each player at the dribble series station, eleven pylons, two baskets, one or two toss-backs or a wall, a whistle and perhaps as many as four stopwatches for the various timekeepers.

Procedure: Divide the team up at the four stations (see Diagram 15.2).

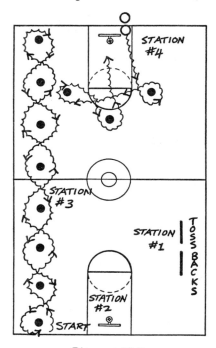

Diagram 15.2

   Station #1: Toss-back drills. Coach decides on drill or drills to be run and for how long.

   Station #2: Free throws (five at a time). Players write their scores on paper.

   Station #3: Dribble through pylons as shown in the diagram. One player goes at a time, and can record times for each trip.

   Station #4: Can run to the right and then to the left for speed. Record times. The drill is shown on diagram.

Time: Total time to complete the four stations will be 12 to 16 minutes (3 to 4 minutes at each station).

Coaching Points: Drills can be incorporated in the practice schedule at any time during the early season. Toss-back drills are generally designed to improve passing skills or reaction skills. If there are no toss-backs available, then any drill previously described in the book that can utilize a wall will suffice. Move players from one station to the next quickly.

ONE-COURT STATION DRILL #2

Purpose: The following skills are emphasized: dribbling and handling the basketball, shooting, jumping, agility, and various types of dribbles with a lay-up.

Number of Personnel: Two to seven players per station, a timekeeper, and coaches to oversee the players at the stations (see Diagram 15.3).

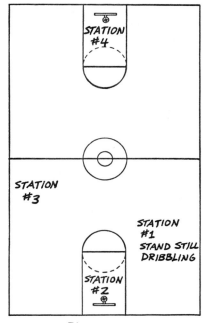

Diagram 15.3

Equipment and Facilities: Two benches, two ropes attached to a wall, two baskets, one ball for the dribble series station, a basketball for each player at the stationary dribbling and the game-shot stations, a stopwatch, and a whistle for the timekeeper.

Procedure:

Station #1: Stationary Dribbling

1. Dribbling across body from outside left leg to outside right leg with low, quick dribbles using both hands.
2. Crossover dribbling from left to right and right to left.
3. Dribbling a figure 8 around and through the legs.
4. Dribbling a circle around both legs with the feet placed together.
5. See Chapter 4, "Ball Handling," for more stationary ball drills.

Station #2: Shooting. Players work on a particular shot for their positions. Record shots made and missed if possible.

Station #3: Two benches.

1. Bench: jump over twenty-five times.
2. Bench: start with one foot on ground, other on bench—jump and reverse feet.
3. Jump ropes: jump gradually up ropes with both feet together and then back down (see Diagram 15.4).

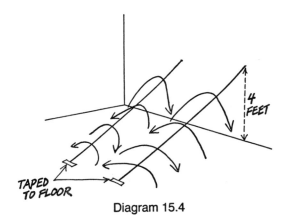

Diagram 15.4

Station #4: Dribble Series. (*See Dribble Series Drill in Chapter 4 "Ball Handling Drills."*) Start right side. Execute following dribbles:

1. Speed
2. Change of Pace
3. Crossover
4. Spin

Time: Each station should run for 3 to 4 minutes. Total time to complete all four stations will be 12 to 16 minutes.

Coaching Points: Drills that can be used in the early portion of the practice season. Coach must have players hustle from one station to the next.

ONE-COURT STATION DRILL #3

Purpose: The following skills are practiced: defensive stance and foot movements, offensive backing down the court dribble, jumping, lay-ups, agility and timing on rebounds, and conditioning.

Number of Personnel: Two to six players per station, a timekeeper, and coaches.

Equipment and Facilities: Two baskets, a jump rope for each player at a station, six basketballs, a stopwatch and whistle for the timekeeper.

Procedure: Divide the team up at the four stations (see Diagram 15.5).

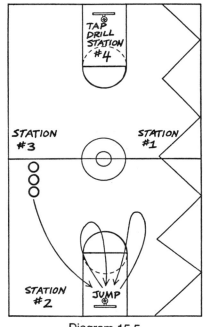

Diagram 15.5

Station #1: Alternate following drill each time through:

1. Defensive shuffle
2. Offensive back down court dribble

   Station #2: Players begin in one line and execute:

1. A running jump off the left foot from the right side

2. A running jump off the right foot from the left side

3. A running jump off both feet down the middle of the lane

Players should try to touch the highest spot on board each time they jump. After doing drill without a basketball, they could do drill with a basketball and create a lay-up situation.

Station #3:

1. Jump rope

2. Jump line for 30 seconds or seventy-five times, whichever coach desires

Station #4: Tapping Drill in pairs (see Tapping Drill, Chapter 13).

Ten straight taps; tenth in

If coach has three players per station, they could use the Ante-Over and Rebound Drill (see Chapter 13, Rebounding Drills).

Note: Each station should run for 2 to 3 minutes. Keep players moving to next station.

Time: 8 to 12 minutes.

Coaching Points: Drills will be most effective if used in the early part of the season. Coach should encourage players to give maximum effort at each station. Players must move quickly from one drill to the next.

EARLY-SEASON STATION DRILLS

Purpose: Players practicing a wide variety of skills: foot quickness and agility, inside power move, the four basic dribbles (speed, crossover, change-of-pace and spin), jumping ability, defensive stance and foot movement, jump-shooting on balance and hand-eye coordination. These station drills should be done in the early season because of their excellent use for conditioning purposes.

Number of Personnel: Up to forty players in pairs, one coach to keep time and change the players to different stations, and at least one other coach to supervise the stations. A coach or manager is necessary to set up the stations at least 10 minutes before drills are to begin.

Equipment and Facilities: Six baskets, sixteen basketballs (possibly less if the number of players doing the drills is greatly reduced from the maximum number of forty), a large wall, tape to mark the floor and space away from the baskets for several drills, a stopwatch, and a whistle.

Procedure: (See Diagram 15.6.)

Station #1: Agility Drill #9, Chapter 1. Four sets of this drill should be set up in any empty space available. No basketballs are used.

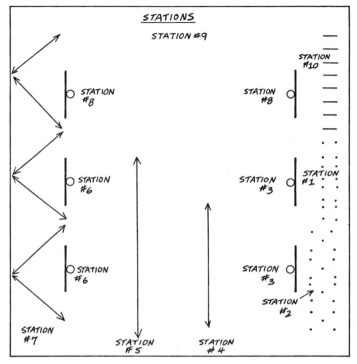

Diagram 15.6

Station #2: Agility Drill #7, Chapter 1. Four sets of these are to be set up in any space available. No basketballs are needed.

Station #3: Power Move Drill, Chapter 9. Two baskets and four basketballs at this station. Two players are assigned to each basket. At the halfway point of the station, the players change roles from shooter to rebounder and vice versa.

Station #4: Seventeen Touch Drill, Chapter 2. Drill can be done in any open area where there are two sidelines of a full court available. No basketballs are needed.

Station #5: Dribbling. Players work on the four basic dribbles—speed, crossover, change-of-pace and spin—in any available area. Each player must have a basketball.

Station #6: Rim Touches—Jumping Ability Drills, Chapter 3. Drill must have two baskets with two players at each basket. No basketballs are needed in order to perform this drill.

Station #7: North Carolina Zig Zag Series, Chapter 5. The coach needs enough space only to do the first part of the series when there are no offensive players used and no basketballs.

Station #8: Two-player Shooting Drill, Chapter 6. Two baskets will be used with two players per basket. At the halfway point of the station, the rebounder and shooter exchange roles. The drill utilizes one basketball per pair of players.

Station #9: Ball Reaction Drill, Chapter 1. The drill requires one basketball for each pair of players and a minimal amount of open space to execute the drill. When the drill at this station is half finished, then players change roles.

Station #10: Wall Bounce-Shuffle Drill. Pieces of tape are placed on the floor 6 to 8 feet apart and about 3 to 5 feet from a wall. A player begins the drill with one foot outside a piece of tape. Player bounces the ball off the wall and shuffles feet so that opposite foot is outside the other piece of tape. Player then continues the process. Each time player bounces the basketball against the wall he or she must get opposite foot outside the other piece of tape. The coach must set up four sets of this drill in any empty space available where a wall may be utilized.

Time: Drill at each station lasts 1 minute. When coach wants the players to move to the next station, he or she blows whistle twice. Coach will also blow whistle once at each 30-second mark for those stations in which it is necessary for players to change roles. The total time needed to complete all the stations is approximately 10 minutes.

Coaching Points: Drills are designed for excellent conditioning and selected skill development purposes. Particularly useful early in the season. They should be done at the beginning of practice. Coach must keep an accurate account of the time. Players should give 100 percent at each station and hustle from one to another.

BASKETBALL SKILLS CONTEST

Purpose: Players practice the following skills in a competitive setting: lay-ups, dribbling, passing, defensive shuffle, jump shots, rebounding, and the inside power move.

Number of Personnel: Any number of players from three to a total of one hundred twenty. A coach is needed to oversee the contest and keep time. If there is a large number of players performing the drill, then there should be eight other people present to supervise one drill each out of the total of eight drills. A small number of players will require less people to supervise.

Equipment and Facilities: Contest requires the use of a gym with a min-

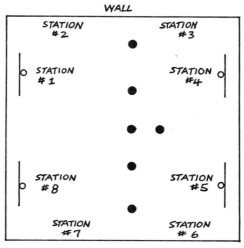

Diagram 15.7

imum of four baskets. The following materials are also needed: eight basketballs, six cones or pylons, two shallow boxes, four whiffle balls, a roll of tape, and a large wall. The person overseeing the contest must have a stopwatch and a whistle.

Procedure: The contest is divided into eight drills. Players begin and end the individual drill they are doing on the whistle. Points are assigned for each drill. The player who earns the most points wins the contest. The coach places players in groups of about equal number according to the number of players who are going to do the drill and the number of people available to supervise. Each drill is described below:

1. *Lay-ups:* Players make as many lay-ups as possible, receiving one point for each made lay-up. They must shoot the lay-up alternating sides on *each* shot.

2. *Shuffle and Pass Drill:* Tape is placed on the floor approximately six feet apart and about three to four feet from a wall. Players must get one foot outside the tape as they shuffle and bounce a basketball against the wall. They receive one point for each time a foot gets outside the tape.

3. *Spot Passing Drill:* A description of the drill is given in Chapter 11.

4. *Jump Shots:* Players try to make as many as they can in a given time period from the fifteen-foot range. They receive three points for each successful jumper. They must go back past the foul line for each shot.

5. *Power Move Drill:* An explanation of procedure can be found in Chapter 9. Players earn one point for each made basket.

6. *Cone Dribbling Drill:* Players try to go past as many cones as possible in a given time period. They earn one point for each pylon they pass. One full trip through the cones is worth eleven points (see Diagram 15.7).

7. *Defensive Shuffle Drill:* For explanation of the drill refer to Chapter 5.

8. *Superman Drill:* Refer to Chapter 13 for a description. Players get one point for each time they get both feet outside the foul lane.

Time: It is recommended that each drill run for 30 seconds. It would then take one player a total of 4 minutes to complete the drills. (If, for example, there were eighty players in the contest, then the coach would place ten at each drill. It would take a total of 5 minutes for all ten players to complete one drill. Total time would then be 40 minutes to finish the contest.) The coach could increase the length of each drill to 45 or 60 seconds, but must realize that will greatly increase the total time to complete the contest. How long the contest lasts will depend largely on the number of players that are involved.

Coaching Points: Coach should try to have a scorekeeper at each station so that the number of participants at each station is lessened. The contest can be an effective means for evaluating players and then might be used to help reduce the squad. Drills should be done very early in the season and at the beginning of practice. The winners (top one, two, or three scorers) should be rewarded in some manner by the coach.

APPENDIX A: OFFENSIVE FUNDAMENTALS

I. Ball Handling
  A. Keep ball low
  B. Control with fingers
  C. Keep body in basketball position
  D. Head up, eyes forward
  E. Be able to use both hands effectively
  F. Types of dribbles
    1. Speed
      a. Get from one point to another as quickly as possible.
      b. Push ball out in front
      c. Keep ball at approximately waist level
    2. Crossover or change-of-direction
      a. Plant same foot as hand being used to dribble
      b. Take other foot in opposite direction forming a V cut
      c. As change hands with the dribble, cross the ball over in front by keeping it low
      d. Push ball back out in front after changing hands with the dribble
    3. Stop-and-go or change-of-pace
      a. Used when coming off a speed dribble
      b. Come to a sudden slow down while keeping the ball under control more to the side
      c. Freeze defensive player, then push ball back out in front
      d. Get back to maximum speed as quickly as possible
    4. Spin or reverse
      a. Plant opposite foot of hand being used to dribble
      b. Swing other foot behind while pulling the ball around 180°
      c. Next dribble will now be with the opposite hand
    5. Hockey step
      a. Come to a stop while maintaining control of the basketball
      b. Bang feet quickly

    c. Use head and shoulder fakes to get defensive player off balance

    d. Use a crossover step and push ball back out in front in same hand as which player wishes to go

  6. Back down the court

    a. Back is to the defensive player

    b. Keep body between ball and defensive person

    c. Dribble with hand opposite the direction desired (if going to the ball handler's left, ball should be in the right hand)

    d. Opposite arm should be up about chest level with elbow bent

    e. Look over the shoulder opposite of the hand that is handling the basketball

    f. Feet should be moving in a defensive shuffle movement

    g. When changing direction

      1. Plant same foot as the direction being taken

      2. Swing other foot 60° to 90° while keeping body between defensive player and the ball

      3. Turn head to look over other shoulder

      4. Place ball in other hand

      5. Opposite arm now goes up to protect

  7. Behind-the-back

    a. While going forward pull ball around back as opposite foot steps forward

    b. Ball continues to be dribbled with opposite hand

II. Shooting

  A. Lay-ups

    1. Concentrate on target on backboard

    2. Extend shooting arm toward target

    3. Jump off foot opposite the shooting hand

    4. Drive same leg as shooting hand up toward basket

    5. Think soft

    6. Jump-stop lay-up

      a. After last dribble come to two-footed stop

      b. Land on balance

      c. Feet should be about shoulder-width apart and parallel with the backboard

      d. Drive ball up to basket using the strong hand

  B. Hook shot

    1. Aim for target—either spot on backboard or back of iron

    2. Ball comes off the thigh of the shooting hand with shooting hand underneath ball and other hand on top of ball

    3. Look over shoulder closest to basket

    4. Arch back

     5. Drive same leg as shooting hand up as in execution of a high jump

     6. Follow through on shot—proper rotation

  C. Jump shot

     1. Form

        a. Shooting-side foot should be slightly in front of other foot for best balance

        b. Feet and body should be square with target

        c. Knees should be bent; flex legs for power and rhythm

        d. Eyes should be on target and not follow shot

        e. Ball should be held on fingers, palm off ball

        f. Shooting hand should be underneath ball

        g. Non-shooting hand must be on side of ball

        h. Shooting wrist cocked

        i. Elbow of shooting arm should be in toward the body and underneath the basketball arm forms a rectangle and ball is off to the shooting hand side of the head

        j. Extend shooting arm straight up on shot; do not let arm form a triangle

        k. Follow through

           1. Wrist comes all the way through after ball leaves hand so that middle finger points down into the bucket

           2. Ensures ball having proper backspin on shot

     2. Shoot at peak of jump or just before

     3. Jump straight up on shot

     4. Shot selection

        a. Never shoot when off balance

        b. Don't take bad shots—experience, coaching philosophy, and point in the game at which shot is taken will determine if it is a good or bad shot

     5. Maintain a rhythm; shooting motion must be smooth (no hitches or hesitations)

     6. As a coach, do not fool with a shooter who is successful

  D. When shooting off a dribble, make last dribble hard

  E. Have confidence

III. Free Throw Shooting

  A. Get in the position which is most comfortable

  B. Do the same thing every time

  C. Relax

  D. Have confidence; see the ball going in before shooting

  E. See Part II, C. Jump shot

IV. Inside Moves

  A. Positioning

     1. Rule: always be on the box or above it

2. Wide base, elbows up, knees flexed
3. Give target for pass
4. Always receive pass with both feet on the floor (can then use either foot as a pivot foot)
5. Be active with the feet in order to maintain position on defensive player
6. Adjust to defensive man
   a. If being guarded behind
      1. Keep feet wide and try to keep contact with defensive player by using the buttocks
      2. Elbows should be up about shoulder height
      3. Knees flexed
      4. Hands up to give target to passer
      5. Move slightly toward ball when pass is thrown
   b. If being fronted
      1. Turn body sideways so that it could intersect the back of the defensive player at a 90° angle
      2. Use the thigh and hip of the leg closest to the defensive player to press against the buttocks to move player off the lane a little further
      3. Place forearm closest to the defensive person at the back of the neck (be sure not to use it to push off)
      4. Put far arm away from defensive player up to give a target to the passer
      5. On lob pass, go after basketball and catch on balance with a two-footed stop
   c. If guarded on a side
      1. Keep body sideways so that it could intersect the middle of the defensive player's body at a 90° angle
      2. Use the closer hip to the defensive person in order to maintain position
      3. Place closer forearm to the defense up by throat area (be sure not to throw it or use it to push off)
      4. Place far arm from defense out so as to give a target
      5. On pass, move toward ball while using body to shield defensive player
B. Types of moves
   1. Power move
      a. Feet should be parallel with the backboard.
      b. Give ball fake
         1. Take ball out of chest on a 45° angle
         2. Raise ball up to top of head level
      c. Jump up and in towards the basket
      d. Use strong hand to shoot

 e. Try to use arms and body to protect ball from block
2. Hook shot (see Part II. Shooting)
3. Jump hook
 a. Turn body sideways so that it is in a direct line with the target
 b. Jump off both feet
 c. Use far hand from defensive player to shoot
  1. Arm should go in a line even with the body or just inside the body line
  2. Follow through on shot
 d. Get closer arm to defensive player up so as to keep defense away from shot (be sure not to push off)
4. Drop steps
 a. Drop baseline foot
  1. Drop foot directly towards basket
  2. Take one dribble with far hand from defense in order to protect ball
  3. Come to jump stop so that feet are parallel with the backboard
  4. Execute a power move
 b. Drop foul-line foot
  1. Drop foot directly across lane
  2. Take one dribble with far hand from defensive player in order to protect ball
  3. Take two steps and head toward opposite box
  4. Execute a hook shot
 c. Can fake a drop step one way by turning shoulder and head (keep both feet planted) and then drop step the other way
5. Turn and face basket
 a. Use one of two types of pivots
  1. Reverse pivot (swing non-pivot foot away from defensive player)
  2. Inside pivot (swing non-pivot foot in toward defensive player)
 b. Pivot on baseline foot
  1. Bring ball up as turning to show the defense the ball
  2. Read the defense
  3. Two moves possible:
   (aa) If defense gives room, then shoot jump shot
   (bb) If defense comes up tight
    (1) Execute a crossover step
    (2) Take one dribble and two steps
    (3) Head for opposite box
    (4) Shoot a hook shot

   c. Pivot on foul-line foot
    1. Bring ball up as turning to show the defense the ball
    2. Read the defense
    3. Two moves possible:
     (aa) If defense gives room, then shoot jump shot
     (bb) If defense comes up tight
      (1) Execute a crossover step
      (2) Take one dribble
      (3) Come to a jump stop with feet parallel to backboard
      (4) Execute a power move
  6. Turnaround jumper
   a. Fake one of the two drop steps by actually dropping the baseline or foul-line foot
   b. In one motion pivot back on other foot to square up to basket and shoot jump shot
 C. When receiving the ball
  1. Keep ball up near chest
  2. Look over baseline shoulder immediately to read defensive player's position
 D. Take what the defense gives
  1. If defensive player overplays on baseline side, then drop foul-line foot across lane
  2. If defensive player overplays on foul line side, then drop baseline foot directly to basket
  3. If defense plays straight up, then look to use a move other than the drop steps

V. Passing and Receiving Passes
 A. Passing
  1. Most important thing is to pick out a target and hit it
  2. Make pass catchable
  3. Learn to read defense
  4. Types of passes
   a. chest
    1. Ball is thrown out of the chest with two hands
    2. Hands are on either side of the ball
    3. Extend arms and follow through—thumbs should be pointing down
   b. Bounce
    1. Can use one or two hands (if two, then follow-through would be same as chest pass)
    2. Pick out a spot on the floor to hit so that ball comes up between thigh and waist level of receiver

    c. Baseball
1. Throw with strong hand
2. Use other hand to help hold ball until ready to release ball
3. Throw off side of head
4. Follow through straight with wrist (do not turn wrist sideways)
5. Used in long-distance passing

    d. Overhead
1. Keep ball over top of head, using two hands
2. Throw and follow through (thumbs pointing down)
3. Generally used in outletting a basketball and/or against zone defenses

    e. Hook or curl
1. Use a crossover to step across the defensive player's body
2. Throw ball from about shoulder or armpit height away from defensive player
3. Can use two hands or one hand
4. Use bounce pass
5. Generally used to get ball into a post

    f. Lob
1. Throwing ball above a defensive player to a teammate
2. Must have proper touch—high and long enough to get over defense yet not too high or long to be out of teammate's reach

5. Use bounce pass into low post players unless being fronted (then may be able to use a lob)
6. Do not be afraid to fake a pass one way and then go another

B. Receiving passes
1. Look ball into hands
2. Always run over toward the pass; meet the ball
3. Use hands as a cushion

VI. Outside Moves

A. Receive pass and get into triple-threat position
1. Do not put ball on floor immediately
2. Turn and face basket
3. Protect ball in waist to mid-section area
4. Ball should be in hip area to the shooting hand side
5. Try to get ball within shooting range

B. Jab step series
1. Always use same foot as shooting hand for the jab step
2. Other foot is the pivot foot
3. Proper form on jab step

      a. Throw it directly at the defensive player

      b. Should be a short, quick step on the ball of the foot

      c. Be careful not to overextend foot (stay on balance)

      d. Use ball to fake an opponent

  4. Types of moves

      a. Jab step–jumper

         1. Throw jab step

         2. Go straight up for jumper (do not bring jab step foot back before shooting)

         3. Used when defense moves backwards to prevent drive

      b. Jab step–extend–drive

         1. Throw jab step

         2. Extend jab step foot past defensive player's feet

         3. Put ball on floor with hand away from defense and drive to basket

         4. Used when defensive player does not move or goes slightly forward

      c. Jab step–crossover–drive

         1. Throw jab step

         2. Execute a crossover with the jab-step foot

         3. Extend foot just outside of defensive player's foot to get the advantage

         4. Put ball on floor with far hand from defense and drive to basket

         5. Used when defensive person overadjusts to the side of the jab step

      d. Jab step–one dribble–jump shot

         1. Throw jab step

         2. Take one quick, hard dribble to the jab foot side or to opposite side after executing a crossover step

         3. Be sure to put ball on floor with hand furthest from defensive player

         4. Go straight up for jump shot

         5. Used when defense goes back on initial jab step

      5. Take what defense gives

VII. Offensive Rebounding

  A. Crash boards consistently

  B. Avoid box-out

      1. Fake and go opposite—before defense makes contact step as though going in one direction and quickly step in the opposite

      2. Spin—attack middle of defensive player's feet and spin around the player by using either foot as a pivot foot

      3. Hook step—lock feet with defensive rebounder in order to be on equal standing

    4. Pressure and spin—apply pressure to one side of defensive player and spin in the opposite direction

C. Keep ball up

D. Taps
    1. Control ball with fingers
    2. Use tap to keep ball alive when unable to control ball cleanly

VIII. Setting and Using Screens

A. Setting Screens
    1. Flex knees
    2. Hands should be on chest with elbows slightly out
    3. Make contact as long as player can see screen (if can't see screen, then must give one step)
    4. Maintain wide base with feet
    5. Must stay stationary; cannot move once contact is made

B. Using Screens
    1. Set up defensive player by moving in opposite direction
    2. Wait for screen—always better to be late coming off a screen than early
    3. Make sure to run defensive player into screen
    4. Be ready to adjust cut or move if defense starts to cheat on the screen

C. Types of screens
    1. On-the-ball or two-player game
        a. One offensive player sets a screen for a teammate with the ball
        b. Player with ball uses dribble off screen to drive to basket, look for jump shot, or a pass to teammate
        c. Person setting screen rolls to basket after contact
            1. Pivots on far foot from teammate
            2. Swings other foot in direction of the dribbler
            3. Puts inside arm up to give target to teammate with ball
            4. Cuts on a line to the basket
    2. Down or front
        a. Both offensive players are away from the ball with one close to the basket and the other on the perimeter
        b. Player on the perimeter
            1. Goes down to screen for teammate
            2. Pivots on inside foot and swings other back to the ball (opening up to ball after screening)
            3. Tries to pin defensive player on back
        c. Player nearer the basket
            1. Comes off of teammate's screen
            2. Gives target to player with ball to look for pass

       3. Looks for jump shot, pass inside to teammate posting up, or drive to basket

3. Up or back
   a. Both offensive players are away from the ball with one close to the basket and the other on the perimeter
   b. Player nearer the basket
      1. Goes up to screen for teammate
      2. If defense switches, then screener seals to try to receive pass on path to basket
      3. If defense does not switch, then screener steps back after setting screen to look for jump shot
   c. Player on the perimeter
      1. Comes off teammate's screen
      2. Cuts hard to basket to look for pass

4. Low exchange
   a. Two players are stationed on the boxes on the foul lane (one on each)
   b. Player on ballside box
      1. Goes away to screen for teammate on other box
      2. Can then possibly seal back to ball by going opposite of teammate (if teammate goes low off screen, then seals back high)
   c. Player on weakside box comes off screen by teammate either high or low to look for pass

5. Screen opposite
   a. Player with the ball on the perimeter passes to a teammate in one direction and sets screen for a player away from pass
   b. Player getting screen uses it to cut to basket or to a spot on the perimeter near the ball for a jump shot

6. Stationary
   a. One player establishes a screen for a teammate
   b. Teammate runs his opponent into the screen on a cut to the basket

7. Pass and go behind
   a. One player on the perimeter passes to another and then goes behind in order to get ball back
   b. Player handing off ball sets screen
   c. Options for player getting handoff
      1. Drives directly to the basket
      2. Shoots jumper either immediately after handoff or by taking one dribble to the side
      3. Dribbles toward baseline and looks to pass to teammate on roll to basket

IX. Movement Without the Ball

A. Always make sharp cuts—V Cuts.

B. Types of moves

1. Backdoor

a. Player comes out toward ball and plants far foot from basket and pivots back

b. Pushes off that foot and cuts back to basket

c. Does not turn back to the basketball

d. Outside arm should be target for pass

2. Buttonhook

a. Player takes defensive player to the basket and pivots on inside foot

b. Swings other foot back to ball to open up

c. Pins defensive player on back and looks to receive pass

3. Square cut

a. Used after a handoff on the foul line extended

b. Player moves to near corner of the foul line and pivots on foot closer to basket

c. Swings other leg back toward ball and opens up on cut to basket

d. Pins the defensive player and looks for pass—gives target with inside arm

4. Dip

a. Offensive player executes a backdoor cut

b. If defensive player prevents backdoor by overplaying, then offensive person makes a quick change of direction to dip in front of defense

1. Plants outside foot and moves other foot in direction of basket

2. Continues cut in front of defense

5. Give-and-go

a. Offensive player with the ball passes to a teammate and quickly cuts to the basket

b. Depending on position of defensive player, offensive person making cut may have to set up defense by faking going away before cutting hard to basket

C. Getting open to receive a pass

1. Take defensive player to the basket on a hard cut

2. Make outside foot (foot closest to the sidelines) the foot closest to the basket

a. Plant it and pivot so as to face back out away from basket

b. Extend other leg back out

3. Move quickly away from basket and give outside arm as target to receive pass

APPENDIX B: DEFENSIVE FUNDAMENTALS

I. On-the-Ball Defense
  A. Stance
    1. Feet approximately shoulder-width apart
    2. One foot slightly ahead of the other—straight line from front of back foot should intercept the arch of front foot
    3. Weight evenly distributed on balls of feet—heels should not leave ground
    4. Knees flexed
    5. Buttocks down so that chin is directly above the knees (stay low)
    6. Head up
    7. Elbows slightly flexed with arms just outside the body line
    8. Hands positioned with palms up
      a. Hands are used to harass player with ball but head should not dip forward
      b. Hands should move in an upward direction when harassing
  B. Foot movement
    1. Feet never touch
    2. Feet never cross
    3. Side-to-side movement—defensive shuffle
      a. Step with foot in the direction in which you are going (if going right, step with right foot)
      b. Opposite foot is used to push off, kept close to the ground, and moved not closer than 12 inches toward the other foot
        1. Do not drag foot
        2. Do not pick feet up in the air
      c. Feet should never be closer than 12 inches apart
    4. Retreat step
      a. Pivot on back foot
      b. Swing front leg behind the pivot foot while still facing forward (never turn back to the ball)

5. Diagonal step
   a. Pivot on foot opposite of the direction the offensive player goes (offensive player goes to left, pivot on right foot)
   b. Swing other foot 60° to 90° by opening up (still facing offensive player)

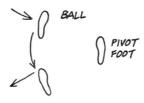

   c. Execute defensive shuffle until offensive player changes direction again
C. Position on Player with Ball
   1. Half-player ahead concept
      a. Try to force offensive player to go in one direction
      b. The up foot in the defensive stance should be outside the foot of the offensive person, which is the direction defensive player is trying to take away (Example: if taking away an offensive player's right, then up foot should be outside offensive player's right foot)
      c. Offensive player's foot should point directly between the defensive person's feet
      d. Shoulder of offensive player should point directly in the middle of the defensive person's body (if taking away right, then right shoulder of offensive player intersects middle of defensive person's body)
      e. Offensive player can go in two directions:
         1. If going to the side that defensive person is overplaying, then defense swings the up foot in the stance back and shuffles to get body in front of offensive player
         2. If going to the side that defensive person is not overplaying, then defense must shuffle quickly in order to place body in front of offensive player
   2. Straight up concept
      a. Defensive player is positioned in a defensive stance to be head-to-head with offensive player
      b. Defensive player must be prepared to shuffle in either direction in order to maintain position on offensive player.
D. Dictate to player with ball; be aggressive
E. Defensive player should be one arm's length away from the offensive person with the ball

F. When offensive player picks up the dribble
   1. Defensive person should get up as close to offensive player as possible without fouling
   2. Use hands to harass offensive player by following the ball
   3. If offensive player takes ball above the head, then defensive person brings arms up and crosses them in front of opponent's face
G. Defense against the shot
   1. Outside jumper
      a. May use one of two methods:
         1. Crowd offensive player by taking a step toward offensive person and extending arms straight up in the air; do not leave floor
         2. Jump straight up and extend one arm to contest the shot—do not leave floor until offensive player leaves floor
      b. never foul on a long-distance shot
   2. Inside shot
      a. May use one of two methods:
         1. Crowd offensive player and extend arms straight up in air; do not leave floor.
         2. Jump straight up and extend one arm (preferably inside arm) to contest shot; do not leave the floor until offensive player does so.
      b. When contesting a lay-up go after block with inside arm (Example: If lay-up is from the right side, then go after block with left hand)
H. Concentration point must always be on the mid-section of the offensive player

II. Off-the-Ball Defense
A. Deny position
   1. Body position
      a. Should be facing the offensive player
      b. Must be between the ball and the player being guarded
   2. Position of arms
      a. Far arm from baskset should be extended out into the passing lane with palm facing the basketball
      b. Inside arm should be chest high with elbow out so that forearm is facing offensive player
   3. Head should be positioned so that defense can see both the ball and the player being guarded
   4. Foot movement
      a. Players must use defensive shuffle in order to maintain position
      b. Two options to defend a backdoor cut:

1. On backdoor cut by offense, use forearm to slow down the cut by the offense and continue to maintain original position
2. Use forearm to slow down cut by offense, but open up to the ball
   - (aa) Pivot on foot closer to basket
   - (bb) Swing other foot in the direction of the ball until it is past the inside foot in order to open up fully
   - (cc) If offense comes back out to receive ball, pivot on same foot and swing other back to get into the original deny position

B. Always be prepared to help out teammates
   1. Further the defense is from the ball, the further the defensive player may be away from the person being guarded
   2. Always maintain ball-you-man principle
   3. Be able to see both the ball and the player being guarded at all times; form a triangle
   4. When guarding a person without the ball, as soon as defense sees an offensive player attempt a dribble penetration, defense moves in the direction of the dribbler

C. Front all cutters to the basket
   1. If guarding person with ball, as soon as pass is made, move in the direction of the pass (jump towards the ball in order to make offensive player cut behind) and make contact
   2. If guarding a player two or more players away from the ball, defense must step into cutting lane in order to front the cutter

D. Front the low post players
   1. Be active with the feet
   2. Attack offensive player depending upon the position in the low post
      a. If low post is below the box on the foul lane, try to attack for fronting position from the foul-line side
      b. If low post is above the box on the foul lane, try to attack for fronting position from the baseline side
   3. Maintain contact with offense when fronting in low post

E. Defense against the pick
   1. Switching
      a. Defensive player on person setting the screen picks up offensive player using the screen
      b. Offensive player on person using the screen picks up offensive player setting the screen
      c. Either defensive person may call "Switch"
   2. Check-and-recover technique

      a. Defensive player guarding the person setting the screen
        1. When offensive player comes off the screen, step out to make offense go wide
        2. Lock other foot with player setting screen
        3. Recover as quickly as possible to guard person setting screen
      b. Defensive player guarding the person using the screen
        1. Fight over top of screen; step over top
        2. Be physical
        3. Continue to play offensive player using the pick
      c. Defensive player on person setting screen gives help to teammate in order to give person time to fight over top
  F. Communication with teammates
    1. Call out all picks
    2. Also call out "help," "shot," etc.
  G. Taking a charge
    1. Make sure feet are planted in offensive player's path
    2. Get body in position
      a. Knees flexed in basketball position
      b. Arms up at chest level with elbows out
    3. When contact is made by offensive player
      a. Fall backward to prevent taking full brunt of charge
      b. Extent of backward fall will depend on amount of contact and momentum of offensive player
      c. Throw arms back on contact after giving a slight push to offensive player to protect from excessive contact
      d. Make moaning sound when hit
    4. When hitting floor try to land on buttocks and slide on floor

III. Defensive Rebounding
  A. Positioning
    1. Distance from basket
      a. Make sure not to get caught too far under the basket
      b. Distance depends on length of shot taken by offense—the longer the shot, the more distance needed between the basket and the defensive rebounder
    2. Boxing-out
      a. Make contact with offensive player immediately
      b. Wide base with the feet
      c. Knees flexed
      d. Buttocks down so as to sit on the offensive player's thighs
      e. Elbows up so arms from shoulder to elbow are approximately parallel to the floor
      f. Forearms extended up in the air, ready to grab rebound

g. Two methods by which to make initial contact with offensive player:
  1. Reverse pivot
     (aa) Pivot on foot opposite from the initial direction the offensive player decides to go (if offensive player goes right, then defensive person pivots on left foot)
     (bb) Swing opposite leg around on an inside path
     (cc) Make contact with buttocks
  2. Front pivot
     (aa) Move same foot as initial direction of offensive player (if offense goes to right, defense moves right foot) directly in front of player so as to cut off the path to the basket
     (bb) Make contact with forearm first, then hip and buttocks
     (cc) Other foot becomes pivot foot
  h. Shuffle feet so as to maintain contact with offensive player
B. Getting the ball off the board
  1. Use legs to drive up to get ball
  2. Extend both arms up
  3. Grab ball with both hands
  4. Be aggressive—go after ball with authority
C. Executing the Outlet pass
  1. While coming down with basketball
     a. Try to take half turn to the outside (if closer to left sideline, then open up left shoulder)
     b. Turn head to look over outside shoulder to try to pick up outlet person
     c. Keep ball up near or above head while keeping it away from offensive player
  2. After landing on floor
     a. Step toward outlet person with closest foot
     b. Keep other foot planted
     c. Execute two-handed overhead pass toward target
     d. If being excessively pressured for initial outlet pass, then take one dribble to relieve pressure before executing pass

IV. **Zone Defense Fundamentals**
  A. React when ball leaves player's hand
  B. Protect against penetration
  C. Keep hands up to limit passing lanes
  D. Use player-to-player concept on ball

APPENDIX C: FAST-BREAK FUNDAMENTALS

I. Three-Player Fast-Break Rules
  A. Person in the middle on the break
    1. Always keeps head up
    2. Never gives ball up too early unless there is a teammate way out in front of everyone
    3. Stops at foul line; stays under control
      a. In middle of foul line
      b. On a particular corner of the foul line
    4. Throws bounce pass to cutters to basket
    5. Makes pass catchable
    6. Looks to pass first, shoot jumper second
  B. Wing players in the break
    1. Fill lanes as quickly as possible
    2. Stay wide—out near sidelines
    3. Make cut to basket at foul line extended
      a. Make V cut by planting outside foot
      b. Cut in a straight line to the basket
    4. Keep eye on ball to be ready to pass
    5. Have responsibilities after the cut to basket
      a. Either to stay on the boxes
      b. Or to cross under the basket
      c. Or to pop back to their own corner looking for jumper
    6. May run to baseline to look for jumper rather than cut to basket
    7. One may go to baseline and the other to cut to basket

II. Two-on-One Fast-Break Rules
  A. Players should stay wide and split the defensive person
  B. Make defensive player cover a larger area
  C. Make defensive player commit before player with ball decides what to do (drive for shot or pass to teammate)
  D. Non-shooter must be prepared for an offensive rebound
  E. Player with ball must stay under control in order to avoid the charge

III. Five-Player Fast-Break Rules
    A. Person in the middle rules
    B. Wing player rules
    C. Trailers
        1. Try to stay behind the ball
        2. Coach must decide on spots they are to go to, lanes to be run, and the cuts they are to make